FROM RAGE TO HOPE

Strategies for Reclaiming
Black & Hispanic Students

Second Edition

Foreword by Asa G. Hilliard III

By Crystal Kuykendall

Solution Tree

Cover design by Grannan Graphic Design, Ltd.
Text design by T.G. Design Group

Printed in the United States of America

Printed on recycled paper

ISBN: 978-1-932127-15-7

Table of Contents

Dedication

To the precious memories of my husband, Roosevelt (Kirk) Kuykendall, Jr., both my parents, Ellen and Cleophus, and my late uncle, Rev. Frank W. Campbell, Sr., who provided me with the unparalleled love and understanding that allowed me to remain hopeful and excited during the most difficult days of my early life. This book is also dedicated to those school officials, social and civic activists, neighbors, health professionals, church folk, friends, caring community residents, and business officials who provided the incredible inspiration, insight, encouragement, and empowerment I needed to realize my hopes and dreams to claim a better future. Importantly, this book is dedicated also to my immediate and extended family and especially my children who have always been and will forever be "the wind beneath my wings." Finally, this book is dedicated to the children, youth, and adults who will benefit from the strategies in this book and those *Merchants of Hope* who will bring these strategies to life.

Acknowledgements

I cannot thank enough the many individuals who were instructional in facilitating the completion of this publication. Special thanks to Jeff Jones, president of Solution Tree (formerly National Educational Service), who first gave me the idea and encouragement to write a second edition of the original *From Rage to Hope.* I am also most grateful to Suzanne Kraszewski, director of publications, for her suggestions and assistance and to Amanda Samulak, managing editor, for her creativity.

However, this publication could not have been completed were it not for the research and technical assistance I received from Kristen L. Hoffman and Kristin McDonald, whose dedication steered the manuscript to completion. Appreciation is also extended to Joycelyn Carr Redcross and Selena Spencer, who were exceptionally wonderful during the early stages of manuscript development.

I also owe a world of thanks to special friends whose ideas and inspiration allowed me to complete this book. Those persons include: Shirlen Triplett, Cheryl Clark, Barbara Tutani, Pam Hoffman, Richelle Williams, Adunni Anderson, Vonetta McGee, Doris Robinson, Bettye Lynn Smith, Sheila Hurley, Brenda Grammar, Diane Pratt, Gayna Evans, Sandra Dolphin, Ulonda Shamwell, Tony Fitchue, and Leonard McCants. For the insight, advice, and encouragement of colleagues Asa Hilliard, Bruce Hare, and Milton Bins, I am eternally grateful. To Ruth Woodridge and Harry Batts, two *Merchants of Hope* who inspired me when I was at my lowest, I extend thanks. To Wallace Charles Smith, Jeremiah Wright, and J. Alfred Smith, who have all enhanced my understanding of leadership, I offer special thanks as well.

Finally, I am especially appreciative of the unconditional love and understanding given so generously by immediate and extended family members who offered insight and support from start to finish. Those persons are Carlene Hawkins, Kahlil Kuykendall Bryant, Stanley Bryant, Rasheki Kuykendall, Ellen and Antar Brown, Eliyah Polite, Yusuf and Rabia Thorne, Peter Guy Logan, Kashif Logan, Mary Helem, Helen Showers, Willie Poston, and Sue Ladd.

About the Author

Crystal Kuykendall is currently president and general counsel of her own firm, Kreative and Innovative Resources for Kids, Inc. (K.I.R.K.). She is the former executive director of the National Alliance of Black School Educators and has also served as director of the Urban and Minority Relations Department of the National School Boards Association and director of the Citizens' Training Institute of the National Committee for Citizens in Education.

Crystal expanded her tremendous love of children and the *Merchants of Hope* who must foster their academic and social development during her years as an educator. A former primary, junior high, and senior high school teacher, she has also been an Upward Bound instructor, university instructor, and a guidance counselor for potential high school dropouts.

Crystal holds a doctorate in educational administration from Atlanta University in Atlanta, Georgia. She also holds a law degree from Georgetown University Law Center, Washington, D.C., and is a member of the Bar Association of the District of Columbia. She received an Honorary Doctorate, the Doctor of Humane Letters, *honoris causa*, from Lewis and Clark College, Portland, Oregon.

Appointed by President Jimmy Carter to the National Advisory Council on Continuing Education, Crystal served as Council chairperson for 2 years.

A gifted and gracious public speaker, Crystal continues to be in great demand as a speaker and presenter. She gives more than 100 speeches annually and has spoken in Australia, Europe, Africa, Canada, and the Caribbean Islands; at scores of local, state, and national conferences; and for school districts throughout the United States.

Crystal is the author of *Developing Leadership for Parent/Citizen Groups, Improving Black Student Achievement Through Enhancing Self-Image, Dreaming of a P.H.A.T. Century,* and *Happiness Is Having/Being a Merchant of Hope.* She recently completed her semi-autobiography, *The Crystal Pumpkin.*

Perhaps her greatest asset in preparing this publication is her tremendous love of children and her belief in the humanity, goodness, and abilities of *Merchants of Hope* everywhere.

Preface

From Rage to Hope: Strategies for Reclaiming Black & Hispanic Students was first published in 1992. I remember all too well the excitement, enthusiasm, and anticipation I experienced as I attempted to develop a book that would not only inform, but also inspire, provoke, and replenish. When writing the first *Rage to Hope,* I felt a bit of apprehension. While I knew I had much to share, I wasn't sure my message would resonate. I wondered if I had the capacity to develop a book that would forever change lives. But the original *Rage* became a best seller. The impact has been worldwide.

My experiences as a primary, junior, and senior high school teacher and university instructor have enhanced significantly my respect and tremendous appreciation for those who choose the incredible profession of education. Yet I have come to realize that many individuals—regardless of life training—can educate, counsel, mentor, inspire, and impact indelibly the development of others. Those who choose to make a difference—to educate, encourage, inspire, uplift, and mentor—are marvelous *Merchants of Hope.*

Much has happened since the publication of the original *Rage.* I've traveled extensively across this great nation. I've heard from countless *Merchants of Hope*—educators; administrators; policy-makers; legislators; civic, social, and religious leaders; parents; students; and concerned citizens. I continue to hold the highest regard for any individual who gives of him- or herself to benefit another. Those who choose to touch lives through the field of education are indeed a special breed. It takes an exceptional person to work daily around children and teenagers who are not his or her own. It takes a unique individual to accept the challenge of teaching. While teaching may be challenging, it nonetheless affords an incredible opportunity to touch lives forever.

The focus of the original *From Rage to Hope* was on the reclaiming of Black and Hispanic students. Yet hundreds of educators nationwide have told me the strategies presented worked not only with Black and Hispanic students but also with youth who simply needed more motivation. Importantly, the original *From Rage to Hope* was utilized by a myriad of *Merchants of Hope* who were not in the field of education but who sought, nonetheless, to make a difference in the lives of struggling students. Without question, the original *From Rage to Hope* provided tips that not only benefited Black and Hispanic students but also students from many other racial and ethnic groups.

In the years since the first publication of *Rage,* our society has become more diverse and the needs of all students, especially Black and Hispanic youth, have become even greater. The original *From Rage to Hope* has impacted many open-minded and committed individuals who share my love for children and concern for the betterment of society. A revised *From Rage to Hope* is necessary now because there is more to share. I've certainly learned more about motivating students. I've witnessed more wondrous works of committed *Merchants of Hope* nationwide and incorporated the knowledge I've gained into this second edition.

Preface

Whether you have read the first edition or not, you'll find that this revised edition will facilitate your endeavors to augment the achievement and facilitate the success of all students—especially those who are Black and Hispanic. Whatever your occupation, you are crucial to the development of children and the creation of a more productive society. Not only do I want you to learn from this book, I also want you to ask colleagues, friends, family members, and neighbors to make use of the information you've learned.

Those *Merchants of Hope* seeking additional insight into the education of Black and Hispanic students will find it in this revised edition. With the addition of more findings, data, and strategies, the chapters that appeared in the first edition are now more comprehensive. The first three chapters still lay a foundation for the implementation of the strategies presented in chapters 4 through 10. The discussion in the early chapters of some of the issues that impact individual and institutional change provides encouragement for those who desire personal and professional growth—not to mention greater school success. The addition of chapter 9, "The Power of Counselors, Mentors, and *Merchants of Hope*," is intended to enhance the effectiveness of those who devote time and energy to youth development, while the appendix shares tools that can be used to enhance the effectiveness of school administrators and policy makers.

Given the importance of all of us in enriching the lives of youth, chapter 11 focuses on the future by examining the actions we can take to help students achieve wellness in all six dimensions: intellectual, physical, psychological, emotional, spiritual, and occupational.

It is my fervent hope that those who read this book will gain the pride, passion, and persistence needed to facilitate school and life success for the youth of this nation. If this revised edition touches just one more life, if only one more child or teenager is motivated to have lifelong success as a result of this revision, if only one more *Merchant of Hope* magnifies his or her outreach, then this endeavor was not in vain. Most assuredly, I remain honored, humbled, and especially grateful for the opportunity, once again, to share.

Foreword

Hundreds of thousands of educators and others who touch the lives of children have been inspired by the riveting speeches that Dr. Crystal Kuykendall has given throughout the United States. I have been privileged to be among the members of her audience on many occasions, and I have long admired her attitude and the intensity of her approach to teaching and learning. She skillfully mixes experiences from her powerful personal saga, her unique personality, and her professional successes and struggles to teach and nurture children as leverage to enhance student achievement. In this revised edition of *From Rage to Hope: Strategies for Reclaiming Black & Hispanic Students*, she uses her rich experiences and research to refine her vision about the purposes, practices, and policies of schools. Readers will be very pleased with this second edition of the immensely popular 1992 original.

Dr. Kuykendall's writing is as clear and passionate as her voice is in her highly regarded keynote and workshop presentations. It would be easy to chalk up her many invitations to speak and consult to her obvious charisma. That would be a serious error because her wisdom goes far beyond her charisma. It is her wisdom that is the foundation for all else, a wisdom that has been forged in the crucible of many challenges that have been met successfully.

From Rage to Hope is the result of Dr. Kuykendall's personal victory over very difficult circumstances. She tells us that she was "born on a kitchen table" in a housing project to a "19-year-old unwed mother" and a proud father who was disabled and poor, with only a seventh-grade education. The poverty that she experienced can have a devastating effect on even the strongest among us. In such circumstances, one must overcome a myriad of obstacles: threats, negative temptations, and even institutional abuse and neglect. I know this poverty firsthand. I also identify with her family's and her teachers' abilities to nurture her in such a way that she never felt defeated. She writes:

> *Perhaps I am also lucky that I didn't find out until I got to college (on four academic scholarships) that I was "culturally deprived," "economically disadvantaged," and "underprivileged." I only discovered recently that I was also "at risk," "latch-key," and came from what now would be referred to as a "dysfunctional family." I was like so many Black and Hispanic youth in our schools today. While others may refer to it as a horrid childhood, few will understand how truly happy I really was. (p. 23)*

To survive under these circumstances, let alone to imagine an optimistic future, can seem impossible, and yet it is a glorious fact that the unconquerable human spirit can do just that. Dr. Kuykendall's life shows that hope can win the contest with rage.

Dr. Kuykendall has focused her special attention on the fate of African and Hispanic students. These groups share a common experience of oppression, including various forms of segregation in school and in life in general. Both share in the experience of cultural neglect, defamation, and distortion. Both live in poverty at a disproportionate rate. Because they share these common elements, sadly, they also share inequities in the provision of educational services. For this reason, Dr. Kuykendall's examination of the pitfalls and challenges of education for Black and Hispanic children is desperately needed. Her wisdom, experience, and examination of the research bring accessibility to what is often an abstract topic. Dr. Kuykendall understands the potential power of schools for all children.

Unfortunately, there is a prevailing historic pattern of low expectations and incorrect and biased estimates of the capacity of low-income ethnic minority students. The same is true of students' motivation and their will to succeed under difficult conditions. These patterns of expectations have meant that educators respond to these children by offering weak educational services that are based on low-level recipes, or commercial programs and educational reforms.

These standardized, minimum-competency programs and reforms are offered almost exclusively in low-income ethnic minority communities. Rarely, if ever, do these programs or reforms yield high achievement. They seem to have in common a failure to ignite the motivation of students and deliver a sense of collective ownership of the success of students by teachers, the community, and the students themselves. They tend to value school management over school leadership— materials, methods, and structures over intellect, spirit, and humanity. Those in the wider community are sidelined as spectators rather than being seen as worthy participants. Teachers are placed in the position of being merely employees, waiting for recipes, assignments, and directions. School leaders keep order while shopping for packaged programs in which they place their faith. No sophisticated research or evaluation is needed to show the low-level academic achievement results that are yielded by such approaches.

These pervasive conditions of low expectations are reinforced by well-respected, elite scholars through such widely circulated publications as Richard Herrnstein and Charles Murray's *The Bell Curve: Intelligence and Class Structure in American Life* (1996), Abigail and Stephan Thernstrom's *No Excuses: Closing the Racial Gap in Learning* (2003), Richard Lynn and Tatu Vanhanen's *IQ and the Wealth of Nations* (2002), and Lawrence E. Harrison and Samuel P. Huntington's *Culture Matters: How Values Shape Human Progress* (2000). *The Bell Curve* and *IQ and the Wealth of Nations* argue that Africans in the United States and on the African continent are genetically inferior to Europeans. Hence, the persisting low achievement results are all that can be expected. *No Excuses* and *Culture Matters* argue that the U.S. and African continental cultures are inferior, and are therefore the causes of low school performance.

Mark Snyderman and Stanley Rothman (1988) did a survey of elite academics for their book on IQ and public policy which shows that the views asserting the genetic inferiority of African children are widely shared. More than half of the elite professionals in the survey agreed that the measured IQ differences between blacks and whites are real differences in mental ability. Similarly, the "cultural inferiority" explanation may be even more widely shared. It is only because our expectations are so low for poor and ethnic minority children that there is little outrage or a sense of urgency about the status quo. We do not recognize the genius of these children. Dr. Kuykendall's arguments provide a powerful alternative to the continuous drumbeat of literature and programs that defame poor children and distort their reality. Her arguments focus on creating the school conditions that make teachers and schools powerful agents of change.

Yes, deep knowledge, good methods, and materials in education matter a great deal; however, it appears that so much of educational reform is the search for a "one-trick pony," a "silver bullet," or anything that does not require us to consider the complexities of a nurturing environment. "Programs" cannot substitute for the humanity of teachers that is the key element to student success. We cannot minimize the place of love, "fire in the belly," vision, values, determination, commitment, hard work, consistency, and strong, bonded relationships on the part of teachers. Less sophisticated, traditional structures and approaches can be used to get high achievement if teachers and educational leaders collaborate to create powerful school conditions.

Good schools are labor-intensive human environments that look more like families than factories. Good teachers and school leaders place a high value on relationships with communities and children. This vision cannot be attained if we remain ignorant of what great teaching and great schools look like.

In this book, Dr. Kuykendall shares herself, her private hopes and fears, and her love of children and education. She also shares her hope and faith in the great potential power of teaching and teachers. This is a major point. In doing this, she issues a challenge to all educators to look deeply into themselves to consider their motivation, values, and will. She challenges supporters of children and educators to look within themselves to examine the strength of their commitment to excellence.

Dr. Kuykendall is a star among stars. She sets the right tone and gives good recommendations that are worthy of professionals who are expected to exercise judgment and to render their expertise on a daily basis. She gives us so much in her robust presentation of information, perspectives, analyses, articulation of processes, and suggested remedies that are precisely the types of suggestions that professionals will find useful. At the same time, because of her clarity, general audiences will be able to understand the job of schools and teaching in a better way. A careful look at the content of this book reveals a very comprehensive view of all aspects of school operations. Many of these topics are forgotten or ignored by school reformers. Hopefully, this book will remind us about the range and depth of what must be done.

I keep coming back to the same position that I have held since before I began my work as a professional educator: my experiences in a family of teachers and educational leaders proved the point that we must examine our will to guarantee that our children succeed. Dr. Kuykendall's work is important for many reasons. Of primary importance is that it makes it possible to re-humanize the dialogue about schools. By offering such a deep level of detail about so many aspects of teaching and learning, *From Rage to Hope* provides a welcome antidote to simplistic, "one-trick pony" approaches to creating excellent educational opportunities for students. The solution is found in community relationships, cultural salience, a focus on self-esteem, an understanding of institutional structures, a focus on motivation, and many more of the topics she addresses in a thoughtful way in this book.

Readers of *From Rage to Hope* will be treated to an authentic look at the real world of schools. They will find illumination, inspiration, and an action agenda, and above all, they will find hope.

—Asa G. Hilliard III-Nana Baffour Amankwatia II
Fuller E. Callaway Professor of Urban Education
Educational Policy Studies Department
Georgia State University
Atlanta, Georgia

Introduction

Either the United States will destroy ignorance or ignorance will destroy the United States.

—W.E.B. DuBois, 1907

Americans should be proud of the tremendous advances our nation has made and the prosperity we have experienced. Even during periods of economic decline, many Americans could still acknowledge, appreciate, and share the pride of citizenry in a nation recognized worldwide as a dominant superpower. Through a study of history and current world events, we are reminded of our indomitable spirit, patriotism, and resilience, and our remarkable ability to overcome obstacles, renew spirits, rebuild, resurrect, restore, and replenish as we bask in the satisfaction of hard-won victories.

However, as proud a nation as we are, with as rich a history of struggle as we possess, and as significant as our numerous accomplishments are, we are, in fact, a nation still in grave jeopardy. Unless we renew our commitment to move beyond our differences, we risk losing our capacity to care and our commitment to provide the most fundamental opportunities to *all* of our children.

Our nation is becoming more diverse as you read this book. We must never allow this growing diversity to limit our ability to grow in humanity. Consider the following developments:

- The Hispanic population has exploded to 35.3 million in 2000 from the 22.4 million counted in 1990—making this group the largest minority group in the nation (U.S. Census Bureau, 2000).

- The Black population has grown from 30 million in 1990 to 34.7 million in 2000 (U.S. Census Bureau, 2000).

- Forty-two percent of all public school students come from these two racial minorities, and most still live in poverty (U.S. Census Bureau, 2000).

The changing demographics of our cities, suburbs, small towns, and rural communities will affect all of us in the years to come. This increasing diversity of our school population will have serious implications for our individual and collective survival.

Educating a Diverse Society

Since the mid-1980s, data have been collected and re-collected on our success in educating Black and Hispanic youth. While the main purpose of education should be to equalize society by diffusing knowledge and directing intelligence to all (Ravitch, 2000), data on suspensions, expulsions, retentions, and dropout rates indicate higher percentages in all of these areas for Blacks and Hispanics and, consequently, more "distancing" of these youth from mainstream America. Public schools, for the most part, have not served our Black, Hispanic, or poor youth very well.

The continued underachievement and isolation of such a large and growing population is nothing short of a national tragedy. Unless more resources are put into the resolution of this crisis, the U.S. will remain a "Nation at Risk." The National Urban League noted in 1992 that Black youth were being attacked by a series of forces that, if allowed to go unchecked, could create a "lost generation." If this generation of children is lost, much of our hope for economic, social, and technological survival is also lost. The problem of educating every generation must be addressed, or we will all share the consequences. As the 21st century began, we found that:

- The leading cause of death among 18- to 24-year-old Black men was murder by other Blacks (National Urban League, 2000).

- The fastest-growing population of homicide victims continued to be Black males between the ages of 11 and 22 (National Urban League, 2000).

- In 1990, the Sentencing Project collected data to show that 1 out of every 3 Black men under the age of 30 and 1 of every 6 Hispanic men of the same age was either in jail, on trial, or on parole. The figure for Black men who are part of the justice system had been as high as 60% in Washington, DC, and 80% in Los Angeles during the 1980s. However, the Department of Justice confirmed there has been little change in the percentages of Blacks and Hispanics in federal penal systems since the mid-1980s (U.S. Department of Justice, 2001).

In addition, we found that:

- The national dropout rate for all students was approximately 25%, but had been as high as 49.6% among

Black youth over the last decade (U.S. Department of Education, 2000).

- Since the mid-1980s, studies have consistently shown that Black and Hispanic youth have been suspended from schools at rates generally three times that of their White counterparts (U.S. Department of Education, 2000).

- The proportion of Black men attending college was still the largest decline of all racial and gender groups (American Council on Education, 2003).

Since 1985, the Center on Budget and Policy Priorities has documented that the largest increases in poverty have tended to be among Blacks without college educations. The number of Black children in female-headed households that are poor is still nearly two-thirds. When those households have Black mothers under the age of 25 years, the poverty rate has been as high as 90% (National Urban League, 2000).

According to the National Council of La Raza (NCLR), Hispanic youth face even more dismal futures if effective educational reform does not occur. Hispanics are still less likely than other racial and ethnic groups to complete high school and less likely to have health insurance. More likely than Blacks to be segregated in inner cities, Hispanic men have median earnings that are still two-thirds that of non-Hispanic men (Perez, 1999).

While these statistics are enough cause for alarm, there are some other disturbing trends that aren't as easily documented. In school districts where dropout rates among Black and Hispanic students are lower, administrators must understand that mere completion of high school by these youth is not enough (U.S. Department of Education, 2000).

The sad reality is that too many Black and Hispanic students are receiving high school diplomas without the requisite motivation to lead enriching and productive lives. Even with their high school diplomas in hand, many students still lack the hope and motivation needed for achieving lifelong success. Far too many Black and Hispanic students go through high school without ever believing they can really make it "legitimately" in a society they feel is against them.

Whether we are losing our youth physically—through persistent dropout ("push out") and expulsion trends—or mentally and emotionally, the bottom line is still the same. When our youth become convinced that they will not succeed academically, when they become convinced that they will not make it in "mainstream" America or even be welcome in mainstream America—regardless of their achievements—they will then take whatever skills and ingenuity they think they possess and seek the "low road" of life. Without the skills and motivation necessary for legitimate prosperity, even high school graduates are likely to turn to unproductive pursuits, becoming easy prey to those who would enlist them in criminal and even violent activity. The challenge for educators is to help more of these youth make it legitimately, on life's "high road."

Restructuring Priorities

Without a doubt, the education of Black and Hispanic youth must become a national priority. Educators have the greatest opportunity to motivate these students to achieve success in school and in life. Despite the nature of this challenge, educators—and especially teachers—must not lose hope.

The research of Ron Edmonds (1980) and many others since then has shown that schools can have a positive impact on the achievement of Black and Hispanic youth regardless of the influence of home and community. In her powerful analysis of failed school reform, Diane Ravitch (2000) notes that too many schools have bought into the myth that only a portion of youngsters are capable of benefiting from a high-quality education. While it is true that a negative teacher can discourage student development, an effective teacher can overcome the negative impact of prior conditioning (Mitchell & Conn, 1985). The reality is that our schools have the opportunity to bring out the best in all learners, and they are mandated to do so.

On average, our youth spend approximately 6 hours a day, Monday through Friday, in our schools. By the time they finish high school, they have spent an estimated 15,000 hours in school. Many children and youth will interact more with the adults in their "school family" (mostly teachers) than they will interact with the adults in their families at home. Through an understanding of the link between motivation and learning, school officials have fantastic opportunities to make the best use of the time they have with their students. School administrators and school board members are becoming increasingly aware of the fact that everyone in the school family (counselors, specialists, custodians, bus drivers, secretaries, aids, crossing guards, nurses, cafeteria workers, administrators, and so forth) has a responsibility to uplift and inspire students—even if their primary job is not to teach.

As a former public school teacher, I know teachers have both the power and the presence to motivate students. An effective teacher can give children, especially Black or Hispanic children, something many of their parents may be unable to give them: hope. With hope, there is reason to look to tomorrow. Without hope, life is meaningless. Without hope, there is greater propensity for negative behavior. When young people lose hope, they often develop anger, bitterness, frustration, feelings of alienation, and in some instances, even rage.

Moving From Rage to Hope

There is a growing rage among too many of our youth that has caused many of us to live in fear and apprehension. Yet this rage can be diminished. We, as a nation, have a chance. We, as educators, have a chance to recapture the ultimate joy our profession can, and must, provide. We can make life more meaningful by motivating all students to experience school success as never before.

Taking Down the Barriers

The barriers to school success that confront so many Black and Hispanic students can be eliminated. How exciting it must be for school officials to realize they have such great opportunities to enrich the lives of children who lack hope. However, the education of these children should concern all of us. School officials must not bear the full burden of educating our youth. Indeed, as noted thousands of years ago by West Africans and documented by former First Lady Hillary Clinton (1996) in her national bestseller, it does, indeed, "take a village" to educate our youth. While teachers may be pivotal players in society's quest to create a well-educated labor force, along with a more secure and prosperous citizenry, it takes all of us—parents, policemen, policymakers, politicians, blue collar workers, business people, concerned citizens, and Americans of all hues, from all walks of life—to raise our children. All of us, working together with educators and schools, can turn the tide of underachievement among the nation's youth. All of us, working together, must prevent the tragic and inevitable consequences that will beset this nation, and each one of us, if we lose any more of our youth to that "low road" of life.

This revised edition of *From Rage to Hope: Strategies for Reclaiming Black & Hispanic Students* is intended to provide information, provoke thought, and rejuvenate educators and others who work with youth. It provides suggestions to those educators who may have the interest and intent, but lack the information they need to make a significant difference in the lives of many of their students.

This book is also for those individuals who share a common concern about the future of our youth and the future of our nation. For those *Merchants of Hope* who dare to make a difference, this book is another resource to add to an existing repertoire of techniques. The ideas presented in this book will help committed *Merchants of Hope:*

- Develop a greater appreciation of cultural diversity and differences among students.

- Develop an understanding of how teacher expectations are formed and how they often contribute to student failure.

- Strengthen the social and academic self-image of Black and Hispanic youth.

- Overcome some of the school-related obstacles to long-term student success.

- Learn more about motivating and monitoring the progress of Black and Hispanic youth.

- Assess the performance and ability of diverse students more accurately.

- Discipline students more effectively and creatively.

- Create the most appropriate school and classroom climate.

- Strengthen the home-school and school-community bonds.

The worksheets in the appendix are intended to facilitate your efforts to assess your attitudes and behaviors as well as those of the youth you desire to reach. Hopefully, the insight and inspiration you gain will only enhance the gratification you feel as you join many other *Merchants of Hope* in reclaiming Black and Hispanic students and thus reclaiming our future.

Chapter 1

Dealing With Differences

There is no one Model American.

—American Association of Colleges
for Teacher Education, 1973

I long for the day when we will be judged not by the color of our skin but by the content of our character.

—Rev. Dr. Martin Luther King, Jr., 1963

The events of September 11, 2001, will forever be indelibly etched into the memories of most Americans. Not only were we shocked and shaken by the very horror of such heinous acts of terrorism, we were reminded, yet again, of our fear of different people, different religions, different cultures, and different values. While many Blacks and Hispanics have long been familiar with the sting of racial profiling, Arab Americans (and those who look like Arab Americans) have now also discovered the acute hurt associated with the victimization and unequal treatment that result from racial or religious bias, discrimination, and prejudice.

Prior to that fateful morning, America was still struggling with issues of racism. Only two generations removed from the marches, murders, and hate-filled crimes against Blacks in the South, America has witnessed a history replete with the lynching, burning, and killing of Blacks all over this country. Moreover, the atrocities of slavery, the race riots of the 1920s, the deportation of Hispanic Americans to Mexico in the 1930s, the detainment of Japanese Americans in the 1940s, and the terrors of Jim Crow from the 1870s through the 1950s are painful reminders of the polarization and racial animus that have plagued this country because of our inability to deal effectively with differences. It is this inability to deal with differences that often leads to injustice, unequal treatment, and in some cases (too many, in fact) even death. Despite the steady increase of different races within this country, there are many Americans who stubbornly refuse to accept—let alone embrace—our growing and rich diversity.

We are all products of our own cultures. It is not unusual for us to see people, situations, and things the way we have been conditioned to see them. All too often, innocently and inadvertently we draw conclusions about others based on prior conditioning and our own limited cultural perspectives. This is especially dangerous in a school or classroom setting.

For example, a teacher raised believing that people who wear glasses are smarter than those who do not, would, inadvertently, engage in behavior that would reveal to her students those feelings and beliefs. Similarly, a teacher raised to believe that an only child is more likely to be a loner and underachiever than a child born in a large family is likely to make inferences and behavioral choices that reflect his belief.

The challenge all *Merchants of Hope*—anyone who enriches the life of another—face is unique. We must be able to step outside of our own cultural orientation so that we can develop a greater appreciation for and a better understanding of those who happen to be different. Most importantly, teachers must be able to embrace the use of a variety of teaching strategies that reflect individual and institutional appreciation of cultural diversity and learning style differences.

In spite of our long-term preoccupation with educational equality (count the years since the passage of the 1954 U.S. Supreme Court decision in *Brown Vs. Board of Education* of Topeka, Kansas), there is still widespread unequal and unjust treatment of some different and diverse students in many of our educational institutions. This apparent disdain of some for diversity and the corresponding low tolerance of others for differences are reflected not only in some teacher attitudes and behavior toward students, but also in the content of classroom instruction, the books being read, the policies and practices of schools and school districts, the role models most commonly presented to students, the way students are treated in classroom interactions, and the assignment of certain students to particular instructional programs (Sadker, Sadker, & Long, 1989).

Inequality in the Classroom

In too many classrooms, Blacks and Hispanics are still being seen as passive, docile, dependent, non-enterprising, inferior, and less attractive than Whites. Children often receive the message (through classroom instruction and teacher behavior) that all a racial minority has to do to succeed in school is to adopt the requisite culture of the dominant society (Dickerman, 1996). Dickerman found that children have been taught to emulate and pay tribute to those who conform to middle-class, mainstream cultural standards of heroism. Individuals whose heroism involved fighting oppression, preserving cultural integrity, or combating social injustices in ways that were not sanctioned by mainstream culture were not to be lauded or, in most instances, even discussed in most school curricula (1996).

Many educators still respond to students who are different in predictable ways—they isolate them, ignore them, retain them, suspend them, expel them, and in far too many instances, they fail to love them or teach them. Two practices that are considered the most divisive and damaging practices in our schools (Olsen & More, 1982) are still very prevalent: tracking and ability-grouping. A quick analysis of the continued and frequent use of tracking, ability-grouping, suspension, and low-level instructing for Black and Hispanic students begs the question we must again ask ourselves: What is the purpose of teaching? How far are we willing to go in providing diverse youth with the motivation and skills they will need for success in a technocratic society?

Each educator will have to answer this question. Importantly, each educator must also understand the consequences of the inability to deal with student differences. This inability will not only impact negatively on student attitudes about the teacher, but it will also most assuredly impact negatively on the classroom performance of the student.

Teacher Attitudes

Teacher attitudes do have consequences. Once teachers develop low expectations and the accompanying negative behavior, they send signals to students that suggest the student is not capable of success in a given subject area. In a study of multicultural high school dropouts, students described their teachers as "unhappy with their jobs, disgruntled, bored, boring, unfair, and sometimes humiliating" (Fine, 1986). A similar study of teacher behavior on the attitudes of urban youth concluded that one of the biggest challenges in the education of these youth was changing the behavior of teachers who were prone to erode student confidence and their fragile sense of acceptance of their peers. Students were likely to go to great lengths to avoid teachers who they felt had placed them in uncomfortable and humiliating positions (Cooper et al., 1979). All too often, there is reluctance on the teacher's part to use educational programs or teaching techniques that will yield positive outcomes and enhance student motivation (Murray, Herling, & Staebler, 1973). The diagram below shows this cycle.

Figure 1.1

Model for Understanding Teacher Expectations

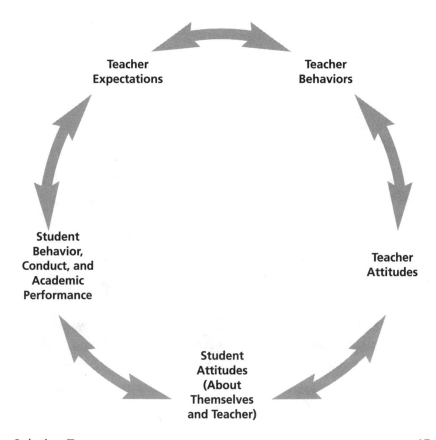

Obviously, the reverse is also true. An effective teacher generally has an attitude brimming with confidence and encouragement. With the right attitude, with a fond appreciation of the individuality, uniqueness, and ability of every student, a teacher can ensure student success. Without such an attitude, there's a dearth of effort, a loss of hope, and an acceptance of student failure.

Those student differences most likely to impact teacher attitudes and expectations are the following:

- Prior achievement
- Prior behavior
- Prior placement
- Socioeconomic status
- Language ability
- Physical attributes
- Gender
- Race/ethnicity

A brief discussion of these critical areas of difference is necessary.

Prior Achievement

There have been numerous studies on the impact of prior student achievement on teacher attitudes and expectations. In assessing teacher evaluations of students, Murray, Herling, and Staebler (1973) found that teachers are influenced by the initial performance of their students. There is even evidence that some Black children receive lower grades than White children—even when they have identical academic performance.

Although most educators know that students learn and grow at different rates, many educators still have expectations that all students will develop academic competencies at or about the same time. Children are often penalized for a slow academic start. Many of these children lose the belief that they will ever achieve skill mastery. It is important that all educators accept differences in growth and development. Such acceptance, however, should not discourage efforts to enhance student achievement. For example, few educators are likely to show indifference to children who are physically bigger or smaller than other children their age. Educators often accept the fact that boys are likely to develop gross motor skills faster than girls, but many educators develop lower expectations when boys fail to develop fine motor skills at the same pace as their female counterparts.

Children "come into their own" at differing ages. Some mature emotionally before other children their age, and others develop certain academic and nonacademic skills before their peers. Too much emphasis is placed on facilitating simultaneous achievement gains. Children who are unfortunate enough to develop responsibility and understanding later in their childhood—or in adolescence—are at a regrettable disadvantage in school if teachers are judging them on the immaturity they showed in their early years. All too often decisions are made about a child's curriculum and school success based on teacher comments (often included in the child's permanent cumulative folder) regarding past performance and behavior.

Such emphasis on differing academic competencies among primary children is not only unfair, but it is also dangerous. Many students come from homes where parents are unaware that they should teach their children how to read and write before they start kindergarten. Many parents have been socialized to believe that it is up to the schools to develop academic skills and motivation in their children. The difference in expectations of what a child should know before starting school is one reason so many youth are being labeled "slow" before they have had a chance to demonstrate their learning potential.

Achievement may also be stymied when a child is in a learning environment where there is incongruity between his or her learning style and the teacher's teaching style. Learning style differences may not affect *ability*, but they do affect *performance*.

Prior Behavior

Not only are many youth penalized for their lack of prior knowledge (as opposed to their lack of ability), but many Black and Hispanic youth are penalized for not knowing how to behave in school or for exhibiting behavior that is too different from that of their White counterparts. The behavioral problems of many Black and Hispanic youth often reflect cultural differences. Cultural conflict and behavioral problems are more likely to emerge when these youth are unaware of expected cultural or communicative norms. Quite often, when the school's cultural or communicative norms are violated, it is considered an act of defiance. Despite the intentions of the students, decisions are made about their behavior based on the interpretation and perspective of those in positions of authority within the schools.

For example, many Black children are enthusiastic and assertive in school when they are required to be passive and non-expressive. Some teachers are likely to react to this enthusiasm by engaging in negative dominant behavior, thereby limiting the mobility, action, exuberance, and motivation of children who thrive on movement and excitement. Such labels as "hyperactive" or "behavior disordered" often are given to these students, even though their in-school behavior merely reflects their out-of-school socialization.

While there are rules and procedures that must be followed, too many teachers have established as their priority the maintenance of order in the classroom. This means that children who are naturally quiet, docile, and unexcited have an advantage. Those children who question and challenge teachers or who display emotional swings are often psychoanalyzed and, worse, disciplined to the point that they no longer want to be in our classrooms or to be productive members of our society.

Students who have previously made mistakes in judgment or behavior are often dealt with unfairly from then on. A survey of counselors in several urban school districts revealed that decisions often are made about guilt in student infractions based on previous student behavior (Kuykendall, 1986). A student who has improved his or her behavior is unlikely to get the benefit of the doubt in many schools. Teachers must remember that every child has a right to be judged based on current situations and circumstances, not on previous mistakes.

Prior Placement

Much has been written and said about the negative impact of tracking, ability grouping, and use of negative student labels (such as slow, uncooperative, unmotivated, immature, irresponsible). As early as 1968, experts were documenting the powerful impact of labels and placements on diminishing expectations in students. Rosenthal and Jacobson

(1968) found that when teachers were told that randomly selected students were gifted, intellectually blooming high achievers, teachers responded with behavior that had a significant positive impact on student motivation, actual classroom performance, and achievement on standardized tests.

Many educators react to children who are different by placing them in low-achievement ability groups and low tracks. One study found that Black children are three times more likely than their White counterparts to be identified as educable mentally retarded and only one-third as likely to be identified and placed with the gifted and talented (Children's Defense Fund, 1985). All too often, Black and Hispanic youth are placed in low-level tracks, ability groups, and special education classrooms when they fail to show mastery of the mainstream culture, when they show a disrespect for school authority, when they lack self-control or an interest in course content, or when they fail to get along with the teacher and other classmates.

Many of the placements and labels often used to describe Black and Hispanic youth are subjective and grossly unfair. Some who are labeled as having "BD" (behavioral disorder), for example, are really exhibiting negative responses to teachers they feel are unfair. Other students (especially primary children) may be unaware that excessive energy, enthusiasm, and excitement are not allowed in many classrooms.

The "LD" (learning disabilities) label also has been overused. While there are children with learning disabilities, the reality is that many of the Black and Hispanic youth who seem disabled simply *learn differently* and must be taught differently if they are to succeed. If a teacher already has a negative attitude about a particular culture or race, the placement of a racially or culturally different child in a special education class or low-ability track will only diminish the expectations of that teacher, thereby exacerbating the problem and limiting the chances of school success for that student (Fair, 1980).

Socioeconomic Status

During the 1970s, there was a great deal of research on the impact of social class on teacher expectations. Decisions about student potential, ability, and performance often were based on family income and status (Cooper, Baron, & Louie, 1975). By 1978 it was widely accepted that the socioeconomic basis for teacher expectations was a contributing factor to the inability of schools to make an impact on students independent of background and general social context (Gollub & Sloan, 1978).

As noted previously, the research of Ron Edmonds (1980) found that schools can enhance student achievement regardless of home influences or socioeconomic status. Yet there is evidence that many educators, administrators, and policy makers still view class and family status/income as indicators of student potential. The use of such negative descriptors as "economically disadvantaged," "culturally deprived," and "underprivileged" indicates the existence of some distorted attitudes and perceptions regarding the likelihood of success for children of poverty. I can speak from personal experience on the need to move away from such damaging terminology.

Once, in a mixed audience of educators and counselors, a teacher complimented me on my academic and professional success. She observed, "You are a true American success." "But," she added, "many of us don't get students like you. Don't you have to admit that you made it, more than anything else, because of your home influence and the foundation for success laid by your parents?" My answer shocked her. While I am fortunate to have been blessed with two wonderful and loving parents, the reality is this:

- I was born on a kitchen table in a low-income housing project (The Brooks Projects) on the west side of Chicago to an unwed 19-year-old high school graduate who would later be a school crossing guard for more than 20 years.

- My father was a seventh-grade dropout who was later honorably discharged from World War II because of numerous injuries that made him a "disabled veteran." He was physically unable to work and lived for all of my life on government stipends due to his war injuries. He finally succumbed to the injuries and received a flag-draped coffin and 21-gun salute at his burial.

- My father was so embarrassed by our poverty that he rarely visited my schools. By the time I reached adulthood, I sought the reason for his lack of visibility. He explained he stayed away for "fear of embarrassing" me. As my hero (all of my life), my Dad could have never embarrassed me. He just didn't know it.

- When my mother succumbed to heart failure and an untimely death at the age of 56, her only material possessions were those I bought for her during my adulthood.

- I never had parents who could help with homework, do science projects for me, or tutor me to do well on the California Achievements, Iowa Basics, SAT, or ACT, or other exams. They honestly believed that my teachers would give me all of the love and support needed to excel in school. Fortunately for me, they were right.

I consider myself very fortunate. I was educated in poor neighborhoods on the west and south sides of Chicago by teachers willing to do whatever was necessary to bring out the best in this poor Black girl. I was especially fortunate to have teachers who were patient, committed, and encouraging. Despite a very slow start, caring and nurturing educators convinced me that I was quite capable of academic and life-long success. I am eternally grateful to those teachers who took the time to mold and motivate me.

Perhaps I am also lucky that I didn't find out until I got to college (on four academic scholarships) that I was "culturally deprived," "economically disadvantaged," and "underprivileged." I only discovered recently that I was also "at-risk," "latch-key," and came from what now would be referred to as a "dysfunctional family." I was like so many Black and Hispanic youth in our schools today. While others may refer to it as a horrid childhood, few will understand how truly happy I really was.

Many teachers will find more gratification when they are able to look past the labels that are affixed to children of poverty. The cycle of poverty that exists in many families can be broken. In their endeavors to inspire and give hope, educators not only help to break such cycles of poverty, they can also strengthen the human resolve of many poor students for personal excellence. However, educators will not succeed until they accept, understand, and build on the untapped learning potential of every low-income child.

Language Ability

In her research on teacher expectations, Sheryl Denbo (1986) found evidence of biases based on language differences. Children who speak Standard English are expected to perform better academically than those students who use non-standard English (Smith & Denton, 1980). Even in situations where Black and Hispanic students had speech performance equal to or better than that of White students, teachers still "heard" them as inferior (Choy & Dodd, 1976).

Many Black and Hispanic youth are likely to start school clinging to the language of their homes, the language of the streets, or the language of their own subculture. Teachers can still show appreciation of different dialects. Teachers who give the impression of racial or cultural superiority only foster the development of an "us versus them" mentality in many Black or Hispanic youth. This mentality and subsequent alienation only increase if allowed to go unchecked.

Williams and Miller (1972) have argued that

> *given the relationship between language attitudes and teacher expectancy, there is the suggestion that with the study of language variations in children, particularly "minority" group children, attitudinal correlates be introduced into the curricula of teacher training to prevent language attitudes from serving as false prophecies, or worse yet, becoming themselves self-fulfilled prophecies.* (p. 264)

In a society as diverse as ours, language differences will always exist. The first language spoken by all of us is the language of the home. One who speaks with an accent was probably born into a home where others spoke with the same accent. If born into a home where the English spoken is non-standard, broken, "Black," or non-existent, a child will learn to speak in that dialect. This does not mean that students who are unable to speak Standard English cannot succeed academically. This also does not mean that children cannot or should not be taught Standard English. It simply means that teachers must respect, not denigrate, the language of the child's culture.

Physical Attributes

Unfortunately, ours is a society where good looks are highly revered. Students deemed unattractive are often ridiculed—even by their teachers. A study of fifth-grade teachers found that a child's attractiveness was significantly associated with the teacher's expectations concerning the child's intelligence, his or her parents' interest in education, the likelihood of future success, and popularity with peers (Clifford & Walster, 1973). While there are many teachers who do not judge students based on how they look, dress, or even smell, a significant number still do. In my own personal observations and informal discussions with teachers around the nation, I am appalled by the frequent negative reference to "funny looking kids," particularly with regard to Black and Hispanic youth.

This failure to see beauty in every child does carry implications for the education and motivation of Black and Hispanic students. There are some Black and Hispanic youth who are likely to see themselves as unattractive based on White standards of beauty. Student perceptions of their attractiveness can affect both the social and academic self-image. Many young girls often turn to teen pregnancy and unsafe (and even deadly) sex just to find someone to love them for who they really are. Educators can augment student self-worth, dignity, and self-love by making students feel that they are beautiful—inside and out.

Gender

It is not unusual for teachers to express preferences for male or female students. The very existence of Title IX of the Elementary and Secondary Education Act of 1965 suggests a propensity of educators to treat students unequally based on gender. The current preoccupation by many with the crisis of Black and Hispanic male children is further indication that these males are not receiving equal, or in some cases fair, treatment in our schools. Gender bias still accounts for diminishing teacher expectations and the poor implementation of effective teaching strategies.

Since the late 1980s, programs have been initiated in some urban cities—Detroit, Michigan, and Baltimore, Maryland, are prime examples—to separate Black male students and to create "all Black male" classes with Black male teachers who can serve as exemplary role models. The intent was to decrease the widening gap in the achievement and dropout rates between Black male and Black female students. Many experts feel this widening disparity was partly a result of gender bias. Some Black educators have even alluded to a national conspiracy to destroy Black boys (Kunjufu, 1985). Whether one chooses to accept the conspiracy theory or not, few can deny that gender bias still exists. There is still a misconception held by many people about the abilities, attitudes, and proclivities for violence of Black and Hispanic males.

Race/Ethnicity

Race and ethnicity are also very serious indicators of bias. The research on the impact of a student's race on teacher expectations and behavior is abundant. Some teachers continue to hold lower expectations of Black and Hispanic youth and reveal these expectations by giving less praise, encouragement, attention, and interest to these youths (Denbo, 1986).

The issue of race will likely continue to be pervasive in American culture, even as we move further into the 21st Century. Each teacher will have to assess his or her own feelings about students who are racially or culturally different. Many educators still believe that the education of Black and Hispanic children is a major challenge. However, the challenge need not be overwhelming. There are many committed educators, but there is a need for even more commitment, sensitivity, and understanding of the academic needs, learning style preferences, and abilities of racially diverse students so that greater numbers of teachers can implement appropriate strategies for improved achievement in Black and Hispanic students.

Dealing With Differences

Below are some tips for giving supportive feedback to all students, regardless of their prior achievement, prior behavior, prior placement, socioeconomic status, language ability, physical appearance, gender, or race and ethnicity:

- Children respond better when eye contact is direct, sincere, loving, and encouraging.

- Children are more likely to modify behavior when comments are directed at specific behavior, rather than at general actions. For example, children are likely to feel worse when they are told they have "misbehaved" than when they are told what specific action caused a teacher to think they were disobedient. When possible, the child should be talked to privately.

- Children also respond better when a teacher's comments are descriptive rather than evaluative. By describing their own reactions as opposed to the student's behavior, teachers are more likely to be seen as supportive instead of judgmental.

- Children must feel that their emotional, physical, and psychological needs are being understood by their teachers; therefore, a teacher's comments should reflect genuine concern for a child's needs. (More will be said about student needs in the next chapter.)

- Comments made to children are most effective when they are shared soon after the behavior. Children are unlikely to remember feedback that is given long after the action or assignment is completed.

- By checking with individual students, sometimes privately, teachers can make sure their comments and feelings are understood.

Promoting Lifelong Success

Once teachers can deal effectively with student differences, they can augment and strengthen the academic self-image and motivation so vital to lifelong success. In order to make sure you are not missing an opportunity to motivate a student, ask yourself these questions:

1. Have you developed a more positive attitude about the potential of diverse students?

2. Are you convinced that you can enhance the confidence of children who have had a slow start?

3. Is the achievement of all students your main priority?

4. Are you willing to explore proven alternatives to tracking and ability grouping?

5. Are you willing to refrain from using stereotypical and negative labels?

6. Can you teach students to speak and write Standard English while accepting their cultural dialect as another legitimate form of expression?

7. Can you look past physical attributes, gender, and race to find the untapped potential in your students?

8. Can you help colleagues in your school or district respond to diversity and student differences in a more positive manner?

If you answered "yes" to all of these questions, you'll find it easier to enhance the self-image of all students and to make effective use of the strategies and activities in this book.

Chapter 2

The Impact of Self-Image on Achievement and Motivation

We cannot possibly bring out the best in our children unless we're willing to give the best of ourselves.

—Crystal Kuykendall, 1989

Since the early 1960s, educators, parents, and psychologists have debated the impact of self-image on the achievement and motivation of children. The development of self-image in Black and Hispanic students is especially significant if we are to prepare them for meaningful roles in mainstream America.

Many scoff at the very notion of enhancing student achievement through enhancing self-image. Some believe self-image is enhanced by increasing student achievement (Ravitch, 2000). Yet, there is ample evidence to show that there is a correlation between student performance and how the student sees him- or herself in comparison to others. For many Black and Hispanic youth, self-image not only affects academic performance, but also affects how they respond in social settings (Kuykendall, 1987).

Youth form their self-image largely based on how they think significant adults in their lives perceive them. Individuals must have a high self-image if they are to cope effectively with the demands of their lives. Unless they feel secure and happy in the present, children are unable to think positively about the future (Gilmore & Gilmore, 1982).

Studies of Head Start programs show improved achievement as a result of efforts to improve self-image (Lazar & Darlington, 1978). Even a study of recruits in the armed forces provided evidence of the importance of self-image in the development of self-control. A study by Little (1968) revealed that progress in learning was attributed to having opportunities to develop self-image and to feel one was participating in a group.

Self-image is enhanced by praise and acceptance and lowered by criticism and unwarranted disapproval. Although there is evidence that older children and teenagers base much of their self-image on the perceptions of their peers, research by Gilmore and Gilmore (1982) shows that this is because these children reach out to peer groups as substitutes for a perceived lack of adult affection. In other words, they turn to peers when their self-image needs are not met by adults. In his analysis of Black youth at risk, Bruce Hare notes, "As early as pre-adolescence, Black children show a trend toward higher peer self-esteem than White children" (2001).

Self-image is shaped and molded over and over again by an individual's life experiences. The building of self-image requires constant renewal and reinforcement. Affection and love are the lifeblood of emotional growth. The small child loses self-esteem when she or he perceives the loss of love and regains it when she or he recaptures that love (Gilmore & Gilmore, 1982). Self-image, whether social or academic, is molded as children derive satisfaction from their ability to do *something* well.

Teachers, schools, parents, peers, and significant others have a critical role to play in the development of self-image in Black and Hispanic youth. Children develop two self-images as they mature into adulthood: a *social self-image* and an *academic self-image.* The distinctions between the two are significant.

The Social Self-Image

The *social self-image* is very often the self-image of the home, the self-image of the playground, the self-image of the streets, the basketball court, the football field, and so on. The social self-image develops as youth relate to others who are a part of the social environment. It determines how individuals feel about their interaction with others in a social setting. This self-image is reflected in how individuals carry themselves, how they speak, how they adorn themselves, how they react in social settings, and how they develop social skills. The social self-image in Black and Hispanic youth is developed through three primary influences:

- The home and family

- The peer group

- Other social systems (such as churches, boys and girls clubs, fraternities and sororities, and structured and unstructured recreation centers)

The Role of Home and Family in Shaping the Social Self-Image

Parents, siblings, and other family members greatly affect how a child internalizes feelings of love and acceptance. The family shapes social skills, personality, and character in the formative years before school. Similarly, a child's perception of his or her physical attributes and nonacademic abilities is molded in these early years as a result of the influences of those within the family circle.

Children who have strong bonds with members of their family unit—regardless of family size, income, or status—are likely to see themselves in the most positive light. On the other hand, children who experience aloofness, excessive criticism, and a lack of love within the family circle are likely to fault themselves. Even sibling rivalry can be damaging to the development of a strong social self-image in some children.

Hare (2001) finds that the absence of fathers in many poor Black homes denies Black youth, especially boys, significant role models and partners in their socialization. Hare notes that since Black parents tend to be harder on same sex children, Black boys in poor, fatherless homes often lose both role models and disciplinarians as they grow older. They are also more likely to gravitate to peer groups as their self-images develop.

The teen pregnancy rate among poor Black girls, a direct result of negative relationships, may also be an indirect result of the influence of fatherless homes. Often, poor Black girls who were raised by single mothers in fatherless homes see motherhood a vehicle for recognized adult status if they have watched their mothers cope successfully as single parents (Hare, 2001). A poor Black girl's self-image is enhanced when she develops positive relationships with other men within the extended family or within the community in the absence of her biological father.

Feelings of love, acceptance, self-worth, and importance often develop in the social setting of the home based on interactions among family members and other adults who are in and out of a child's home. It should be emphasized here that poverty by itself is not a cause of low social self-image. In fact, many poor Black and Hispanic youth have strong bonds of affection with adults within the family circle and are more likely to have stronger feelings of self-worth than their counterparts from more affluent homes, if the affluent home is characterized by condescension and criticism. In my case, my family and my neighbors were poor, but we discovered early that, for us, *Black love was truly Black wealth.*

The Role of Peer Groups in Shaping the Social Self-Image

Renowned Black psychologist Alvin Poussaint found that like most other humans, Black and Hispanic youth have strong needs for acceptance, affection, appreciation, approval, and achievement (Bell, 1985). When legitimate adults do not meet their needs, Black and Hispanic youth often seek to satisfy these needs through relations with peers or adults who are part of the street cultures of their communities. Popular rapper Tupac Shakur addressed this reality in one of his songs of Black urban life when he wrote that as a young boy he "hung out with dope dealers and thugs, for even though they sold drugs, they still gave a little brother love" (Shakur & Pizzaro, 1995).

Thus, Black and Hispanic youth are likely to be especially loyal to those who show an acceptance of their shortcomings, appreciation of their strengths, and approval of their unique talents and abilities. Very often, these needs are satisfied in peer groups where rapport is established and bonds are made. In a comparative study of self-perceptions among Black girls and boys, Bruce Hare found that the self-image of Black boys depends on nonacademic factors such as social ability and peer acceptance. These boys are more likely than their White counterparts to value social skills such as popularity, dancing, sports competition, and rapping, while the self-image of Black girls is still related more strongly to academic achievement (Hare, 1979; 2001).

It is very often through the acceptance of the peer group that many Black and Hispanic youth develop their behavioral norms. The way many Black and Hispanic youth talk, walk, dress, dance, play competitive sports, rap, exhibit sexuality, become street-wise, and even "play the dozens"[1] with one another reflects the extent to which they have internalized their self-worth and place within their peer group subculture. How they see themselves within the context of peer relations is very important to their social development. When peers provide affection, appreciation, and approval, they often become the primary support unit. The older Black and Hispanic youth become, the more likely it is that their values and behaviors will be influenced by peers when other adults fail to satisfy their needs for affection, appreciation, approval, and achievement. All too often, the maintenance of a positive ego and requisite self-respect for Black and Hispanic teens

---

[1]"Playing the dozens" (also called "jonin," "frontin," or "signifyin") is an art in most Black communities because it requires emotional control, creative thinking, mental agility and quickness, and a sense of humor. It usually involves two males (or females) in a verbal showdown where both take turns making negative and derogatory statements, which most often are not intended to show disrespect, about each other or some member of the other person's family—often the mother. For example, "Your mama is so fat that when she jumped in the air she got stuck." The dozens is usually played before an audience of peers who laugh and express some indication of who they think is winning. Even though there are rare instances where the two players may resort to fighting, most see it as a playful "duel" where they can show off a skill and avoid physical contact. Even when youth are aggressive and loud when playing the dozens, teachers should understand it does not necessarily mean they are preparing for a fight. Students should not be disciplined unfairly for engaging in this ritual.

requires the support and solidarity of peer associations in the absence of other supportive adult relations.

The Role of Other Social Systems in Shaping the Social Self-Image

Within both the Black and Hispanic communities, there are significant social systems, such as churches, boys and girls clubs, fraternities and sororities, and structured and unstructured recreation centers. Many Black youth who are given significant roles to play in the Black church (through membership in church organizations and participation in skits, plays, and other church events) develop strong bonds and a positive social self-image. Similarly, Hispanic youth who bond with adult community figures through organized recreational and social activities where their self-worth is proclaimed are also likely to develop strong social self-images.

When family bonds and relations with other peers and adults are positive, Black and Hispanic youth benefit. However, even when relationships lead to negative behavior (as they do with violent gangs or antisocial activities such as crime), youth are still likely to maintain strong social self-images because their desires for affection, appreciation, loyalty, support, and achievement have been met. Educators must remember the power of achievement in the development of both the social and the academic self-image. When it does not appear that Black and Hispanic youth will find approval and achievement in the school setting—or on life's "high road"—they take all of their ingenuity and social prowess with them as they seek success on life's "low road."

Chapter 9, "The Power of Counselors, Mentors, and *Merchants of Hope*," provides more information on the roles that adult mentors and counselors can (and must) play in socializing Black and Hispanic youth and in minimizing the impact of negative peer cultures on their growth and development. When adult *Merchants of Hope* outside of the home come into the lives of Black and Hispanic youth, they can significantly improve how these youth see themselves. Caring adults can minimize the impact of hostile and negative peers on the aspirations of many Black and Hispanic youth.

The Academic Self-Image

Bruce Hare (1979; 2001) notes the existence of a progressive shift in motivation and attachment from the school to peers among many poor Black youth, especially after early adolescence. As youth flee from failure and ego-destroying experiences in classrooms, they seek success in those social arenas where they feel success is most likely. While very powerful, the social self-image alone does not indicate the likelihood for future success in a high-tech society. Nor does the social self-image determine the extent to which Black and Hispanic youth are likely to be motivated to achieve success in schools or in mainstream America. It is the academic self-image that dictates how well children will fare in a society where survival requires higher-order thinking skills and other academic competencies. It is not unusual for some children and teens to display a positive social self-image within their homes, churches, and communities and a commensurate negative academic self-image in educational environments.

The academic self-image is molded in our classrooms. In 1971 Charles Silberman found that 80% of Black children have positive self-images when they enter school, 20% still do by the fifth grade, but only 5% do by their senior year in high school. In a 1985 study of the progressively decreasing scores of Black students on Comprehensive Tests of Basic Skills in the

District of Columbia Public Schools, Bell found that, as Black children mature, they begin to experience many hostilities imposed by the majority culture. Such hostilities often are rooted in the inability of teachers to augment the academic self-image of these youth. While peer groups often succeed in providing avenues for achievement and demonstrated competence through a host of social, athletic, and street-related activities, these relationships offer little hope for lifelong or academic success unless they also enhance the academic self-image of Black and Hispanic youth. Importantly, the peer cultures of many Black and Hispanic teens, while enhancing their social self-images, often carry the danger of pulling these teens into self-destructive worlds of crime, drugs, and sexual promiscuity.

It is the responsibility of schools and educators to develop a positive academic self-image for Black and Hispanic youth. The key ingredient for improving the academic self-image of all youth is accomplishment. An academic environment that offers encouragement, praise, and the opportunity for accomplishment will promote the development of a positive academic self-image (Mitchell & Conn, 1985). Children who are without significant opportunities for in-school success are likely to feel frustrated and inept. However, since the need for accomplishment (of any kind) is so great, many students who are denied in-school success will seek accomplishment outside of school—even if it is through illegal or unacceptable behavior. When educators provide academic experiences that are defeating and discouraging, they succeed only in destroying or debilitating the academic self-images of their Black and Hispanic students. Levin and Schutze (1983) found that teachers who have negative attitudes toward their Black and Hispanic students contribute to the educational failure of these youth.

Educators and school officials must build on the social strengths and skills of Black and Hispanic students in order to build their confidence and enhance their academic self-image. Martin (1980) found that the focus by teachers on student strengths made students feel more confident, thereby enhancing a positive self-image. Even when the student's nonacademic strengths are viewed as negative, teachers must still acknowledge and build on those skills in their endeavors to enhance the academic self-image of their students. When children are successful at something, their confidence rises.

During my early years of elementary school, I not only suffered from self-doubt in academic settings, I also sought support from classmates through negative social behavior. I was the classic talker who could not complete class work because of an inability to finish conversations with classmates so I could focus on assignments. A wise fifth-grade teacher, Mrs. Ruth Odom, gave me opportunities to develop my talking skills and do extra credit work on public speaking. She made me believe that the talking skills I possessed would lead to a prosperous future if I could just make it out of the fifth grade. I'm so glad I listened to Mrs. Odom! Teachers can augment the academic self-image by identifying and developing some of the unique cultural and social strengths Black and Hispanic youth bring to the classroom. An understanding of how the social self-image can be used to bolster the academic self-image is critical.

Table 2.1 provides a partial listing of characteristics of low academic self-image and high social self-image that many Black youth, especially boys, are likely to display in tandem (Kuykendall, 1989). The responses are those provided most often by more than 2,000 teachers surveyed between 1984 and 1987.

Table 2.1

Low Academic Self-Image and High Social Self-Image

Characteristics of Low Academic Self-Image

- Failure to complete work
- Hostility, disruptive behavior, or defiant speech in class
- Daydreaming, poor attention span
- Little or no eye contact
- Frequent use of excuses
- Fear of failure and of trying
- Repeated and deliberate tardiness and absences
- Lack of volunteering or participation
- Tendency to be withdrawn and isolated
- Dislike for school and/or the teacher
- Facial expressions and body movement showing visible pain, frustration, and anxiety

Characteristics of High Social Self-Image

- Confidence in performing before others
- Unique ability in social skills such as sports, dancing, or rapping
- A mutually supportive system with other peers
- The exhibition of a keen interest in and a preoccupation with and persistence in performing social activities such as listening to music, dancing, sports, art, card playing and so on
- Nonverbal communication and eye contact with others, especially when there is familiarity, as there often is with friends and family. This reflects self-assuredness in being able to communicate to those in the friend or family circle without saying a word.
- Desire to succeed in social functions and be noticed by others
- Extensive desire to interact with those who are most encouraging and supportive
- Friendly, sincere behavior
- Facial expressions and body movements that reflect enjoyment

Many teachers and school officials have observed the indicators and characteristics of low academic self-image presented in Table 2.1. What is needed most, however, is an understanding of why these characteristics exist. The following 10 indicators and their causes provide more insight (Kuykendall, 1989).

Failing to Complete Work

Children who fail to complete work often have either a fear of failure ("I won't get a passing grade anyway") or a fear of success. They consequently lack the desire to do well—usually because the need for approval will still not be met. Some children may simply lack interest in the subject area.

Behaving With Hostility and Defiance

Children who are hostile, disruptive, delinquent, and/or defiant in speech in the presence of teachers actually have a fear of other people. Their hostility is part of a warped rationale—"Do unto others before they get the chance to do unto you." Often, these children have been mistreated and emotionally abused. They are hostile as a means of protecting themselves from additional hurt. All too often, the hurt is exacerbated in a classroom that does not emphasize student strengths or by teachers who have negative expectations.

Paying Poor Attention

Children who daydream or show a poor attention span are not motivated to succeed and in many cases are not interested in what is being taught. They either think they are going to fail—even if they do pay attention—or are not inspired by teachers, peers, or parents to succeed. Some younger children may be unaware of the importance of school and the need to pay attention. Some children who display poor attention spans may have real learning disabilities that must be addressed through special teaching techniques.

Failing to Make Eye Contact

Children who have little or no eye contact may be socialized to think that direct eye contact is a sign of disrespect—particularly if the speaker is an adult. However, if no such cultural socialization is evident, little or no eye contact usually indicates a fear of people. Very often the child may not look adults in the eye because he sees dislike for him in their eyes. When there is no real love, direct eye contact makes it more obvious. Many Black youths who are especially proficient in nonverbal communication will detect, or think they have detected, bias in their teacher's eyes, making eye contact with that teacher even more painful.

Making Excuses

Children who frequently use excuses to justify poor performance are afraid of what others (teachers) think of them. These children often need a crutch to justify what they fear most—failure. They have been made to feel inferior but are still fighting against what they perceive to be a teacher's negative impressions. In making excuses, they are actually trying to hold onto some semblance of dignity. This is merely an endeavor to save face, or to assuage their feelings of inadequacy.

Giving Up Too Easily

Children who are afraid to try and who give up too easily generally have a fear of failure. They have already determined that the best way to prevent the pain of not doing well is to abstain from making the attempt. All too often, student confidence has not been built adequately, and the result is an unwillingness to try. Children who have a sense of purpose, who feel motivated, and who know others believe in them will eventually lose this characteristic. By the same token, children who give up too easily and do not persist also have a fear of failure. They lack the confidence to keep going because they really do not feel they will meet with success.

Being Intentionally Tardy or Absent

Children with repeated and deliberate tardiness or absences may have such a fear of failure or a fear of people that they will do anything to avoid being in a situation where embarrassment, pain, or failure is imminent. Cutting class or ditching school is one way to avoid the pain of being in unbearable situations. Some children are absent or tardy for reasons beyond their control. Therefore, this analysis does not apply to those youth who do not intentionally have poor attendance. Some children are tardy because of other extenuating circumstances. For example, an older child may be responsible for getting a younger sibling to class on time and may be unable to make it to his or her own class by the time the bell rings.

Not Volunteering or Participating

Children who do not volunteer or participate may fear failure or success. If they have not been motivated to succeed, volunteering and participating are unattractive. If they fear ridicule for wrong answers or actions, volunteering is practically prohibitive. In addition, many Black and Hispanic youth do not volunteer if they do not feel a teacher expects (or wants) this from them.

Withdrawing Into Isolation

Children who tend to be withdrawn and isolated often behave this way when not treated with respect and confidence. They have a fear of people and may find interaction with others, in what they perceive as a hostile school environment, threatening and painful. Disparities in class, race, and culture between student and teacher can often create such feelings of isolation.

Disliking School or Teachers

Children who dislike school or the teacher will eventually develop such a painful hostility for, or fear of, the school or that teacher that they withdraw from the learning process over time.

Teachers can bolster the academic self-image of their students when they acknowledge positive approval, acceptance, and appreciation of some of the students' social skills and strengths, even when these strengths have been displayed in a negative or disruptive manner. Because the academic self-image of Black and Hispanic students is vital to their academic success, teachers must work hard to ensure that these students have positive experiences in school.

Remember, Black youth may be taught at home to appreciate certain skills that are not always valued in classrooms and that do not reflect the school's norms. These include nonverbal communication, dance and rhythmic movements, learning through cooperation, and verbal interplay during instruction. Black and Hispanic youth may also acquire social "survival" strategies similar to the behavior of others in their communities and culture (hip walking styles, expressive movements, use of Spanish slang, or use of Black English). This duality between the culture of the school and the culture of the family and community can account for much of the discrepancy between academic and social self-concept.

Creating Opportunities for Success

Educators who endeavor to motivate Black and Hispanic students must recognize that both the school environment and teacher behavior can contribute to either the development or the alleviation of these characteristics. Quite often, these characteristics indicate a fear of, or intimidation by, other people. Children experiencing these emotions may do things to give people a reason to dislike them. Many of these youth develop a defensive attitude that often leads to distrust, disdain, defeatism, and hostility. On the other hand, some other youth may go to great extremes to win approval and affection. It is so important for teachers and school officials to understand that many children exhibiting these characteristics have been emotionally bruised. Sensitive to even the most unintentional slights, and well aware of the existence of racism, sexism, and classism, many of these youth are only seeking to prevent additional emotional pain.

As educators augment their understanding of the symptoms of low academic self-image, they can take requisite steps to provide students with other opportunities for school success. The next chapter discusses some of the institutional barriers to achievement that must be overcome in order to reclaim Black and Hispanic students. Chapter 4 then offers a variety of strategies for removing these obstacles, and Chapter 5 offers specific suggestions for motivating Black and Hispanic students in school.

Chapter 3

Institutional Barriers to Student Achievement

Unfortunately, many . . . teachers . . . share the general belief of educators and the public that racial differences in intelligence were innate, real, and fixed.

—Diane Ravitch, 2000

Recent reports released by the U.S. Department of Education on student performance on the National Assessment of Educational Progress (NAEP) tests in reading and science have caused considerable dismay among many educators and parents in the United States. Despite significant investments in education, average scores for fourth graders on the NAEP have held almost steady since 1992 (Fletcher, 2001). Similarly, the performance of twelfth graders on the NAEP science test given in 2000 to a nationally representative sample of school children was slightly worse than 1996 results. These test results show that more than 80% of the nation's high school seniors lack proficiency in science. The results add to concerns that U.S. students are becoming weaker in subjects that are increasingly more important to America (Fletcher, 2001).

Many who examine the academic achievement of Black and Hispanic students conclude that most of these youth are trapped in schools that provide sub-par educations and foster low expectations for their academic achievement (Bailey, 2001). In her highly lauded book, *Left Back: A Century of Failed School Reforms,* Diane Ravitch (2000) proclaims that all students have the capacity to learn and all are equally deserving of a solid liberal arts education. Yet, notes Ravitch, the traditional educational system has not lived up to its promise of quality education for *all* Americans.

Public education is still the best hope and the most promising option we have for the education of *all* youth. While some tout the advantages of private and religious schools, and others proclaim the need for voucher programs and more charter schools, I strongly believe that public education still offers the most options for academic achievement and lifelong success for children of *all* races and economic levels. Public schools can make a difference, but only if those practices and programs that stymie student success are eliminated. There are, indeed, many school-related obstacles that preclude teaching prowess and satisfactory student performance. There are institutional barriers that must be brought down if public schools are ever to live up to their promise. Thus, while many teachers will have to change their attitudes and behaviors with regard to teaching and motivating diverse students, schools and educational agencies, administrators, and policy makers will have to change as well. They must work to eradicate institutional racism and its harmful effects on student success.

Institutional Racism

Psychologist Beverly Daniel Tatum, in her acclaimed book, *Why Are All the Black Kids Sitting Together in the Cafeteria?* (1997), observes that racism, like other forms of oppression, is not only a personal ideology based on racial prejudice, but "a system involving cultural messages and institutional policies and practices as well as the beliefs and actions of individuals" (p. 7). She notes further that racial prejudice, when combined with social power (access to social, cultural, and economic resources and decision making), leads to the institutionalization of racist policies and practices. The Commission for Racial Equality found that if racist consequences accrue to institutional laws, customs, or practices, the institution is racist whether or not the individuals maintaining those practices have racial intentions. *Institutional racism,* therefore, is racism that covertly or overtly resides in the policies, procedures, operations, and culture of public or private institutions, reinforcing individual prejudices and being reinforced by them in return (Sivanandan, 1999).

The existence of institutional racism in our society and our schools must not be ignored. It can be subtle, but it is pervasive. Its very existence can encourage teacher behavior and organizational norms that serve only to reinforce low motivation, underachievement, and poor school and life success in many Black and Hispanic youth.

Often difficult to recognize, institutional racism can be covert, indirect, and sometimes unconscious. The origins of institutional racism are in our most established and respected institutional norms, societal values, and beliefs. This prejudice against groups of people is based on the belief that members of some racial groups are better and therefore more deserving than others. When some students are denied access to opportunities that others have for rising in the class system, they are victims of institutional racism. Racist beliefs provide the foundation for extending unique rights, opportunities, and privileges to the race deemed superior while withholding the same from races believed to be inferior. This prejudice against groups of people is based on the belief that members of some racial groups are unequal genetically and therefore inferior. There can be no equal access to educational opportunities when students are prejudged based on their race and class.

The Council on Interracial Books for Children, Inc., in its "Fact Sheet on Institutional Racism" (1984), declared that institutional racism exists in economic, government, housing, health industry, media, and educational institutions. The existence of institutional racism in our schools creates situations in which many Black and Hispanic students are enrolled in less challenging educational programs—programs that are less likely to lead to the development of high-order cognitive skills and abilities. Moreover, the existence of institutional racism creates an atmosphere in which Black and Hispanic students receive the message that they cannot succeed (Hammond, 1985).

Studies in *The Journal of Negro Education* found that both Black and White teachers perceived that schools and schooling valued neatness, conformity, particular concepts of beauty or appearance, attitudes, language, and behavior. Both White and Black teachers viewed Black males as most negatively "different" from the valued characteristics and White females as the most positive (Washington, 1982).

In an analysis of the impact of institutional racism on Black youth, Howard (1985) found a subtle, often subconscious cycle of self-doubt and, in some instances, an avoidance of intellectual competition. Howard concluded that Black youth respond negatively even to rumors of inferiority. These rumors, myths, and innuendoes have a strong subliminal effect on the aspirations and academic achievement of many Black and Hispanic youth. Thus, by early adolescence, many of these students are convinced that academic achievement will not improve their status or benefits. These students learn to adapt to this perceived definition of reality by giving less time and energy to schoolwork. It should not be surprising, therefore, that the longer Black youth stay in school, the farther they fall behind the academic achievements of their White counterparts (Berube, 1984).

Graves (1978) observed that institutional racism brands Black children as inferior from birth. Knowles and Prewitt (1969) found that within our educational apparatus, Black students suffer from institutional discrimination in many ways, but particularly in I.Q. testing, tracking, classroom ability grouping, and negative teacher attitudes. As Banks and Grombs (1972) concluded, the end result of institutional racism is a steady decline in the academic performance of most Black youth.

Ravitch (2000) found that as late as the 1990s, there were still those who insisted that the schools should not even attempt to educate all children at a high level, that doing so was neither necessary nor wise because society did not need an over-educated workforce and might not have enough uneducated people to do menial labor. Ravitch notes that such worries echoed the anti-democratic views of David Snedden, John Franklin Bobbitt, and W. W. Charters who expressed in the early 20th Century their desire that public schools train children for their different niches in the occupational structure and avoid wasting the public's money by attempting to educate those who were unlikely to attend college and enter the professions.

Indeed the prevalence of so many underqualified teachers in schools that are predominantly Black, Hispanic, and poor (as evidenced by free lunch percentages) suggests that the public schools often provide the worst education to those with the greatest need. A 1996 report by the National Commission on Teaching and America's Future found the following percentages of underqualified (lacking a major or minor in the field) teachers in high school classrooms:

Math

25% of teachers in schools with less than 20% free lunch were underqualified.

40% of teachers in schools with greater than 49% free lunch were underqualified.

Science

14% of teachers in schools with less than 20% free lunch were underqualified.

20% of teachers in schools with greater than 49% free lunch were underqualified.

English

19% of teachers in high school classrooms with less than 20% free lunch were underqualified.

31% of teachers in districts with greater than 49% free lunch were underqualified.

Social Studies

16% of all teachers in schools with less than 20% free lunch were underqualified.

18% of all teachers in schools with greater than 49% free lunch were underqualified.

Hare (2001) and others have called such placement of underqualified teachers in poorer schools "structured educational failure" for youth (or "failure by design"), which serves to legitimize sub-par job qualifications and eliminate legal recourse by students and their parents.

Addressing Institutional Racism

While there have been some attempts to address institutional racism in our schools, much more can be done. In the 1973 decision by U.S. District Court Judge Sarah T. Hughes in the precedent-setting case of *Hawkins v. Coleman,* the Dallas Public Schools were ordered to "eradicate all vestiges of institutional racism from the school system." The court called for extensive training of teachers and counselors along with "institutional and structural changes" in the Dallas Public Schools. Specifically, the judge concluded that institutional racism can be reduced through efforts to increase teacher expectations and by providing tests and textbooks that accurately represent all ethnic and multicultural groups.

Unless attempts are made to eliminate institutional racism, the ultimate mission of public education will remain obscured. Questions will still center on who is to be educated, what they are to learn, and what schools should and should not do for which races and classes. Therefore, public school policy must provide the parameters by which institutional racism can be eliminated. Legislators at the local, state, and national levels must develop legislation that can facilitate the eradication, not the enhancement, of institutional racism. Otherwise, school policy and educational legislation become institutional barriers rather than institutional bridges to student success.

Impact on Policy and Legislation

First and foremost, school district policy reflects the wisdom of school officials faced with the task of determining how best to achieve certain goals and objectives. Before policy can be developed, officials must ask, "If children are really the material interest of this district, how might we provide optimum opportunities for their academic success?" Policy then becomes a set of procedures that have been developed based on the needs of those "material interests." Effective school district policy must guide present and future decision makers by allowing for the selection of a definite course of action or method of action from many different alternatives (some of these alternatives are discussed in chapter 5).

All too often, school policy reflects the discriminatory assumptions of society. All of us frequently act in ways that are socially acceptable. Yet much of our "socially acceptable" behavior actually reflects long-standing discriminatory assumptions and practices. Whenever these practices become embedded in school systems, they are more likely to be perpetuated (Knowles & Prewitt, 1969).

Table 3.1 (page 55) provides examples of different socially acceptable behaviors that are based on discriminatory assumptions and institutional policies or practices that demean or restrict Black and Hispanic youth.

The following findings promote better and more responsive school policy (Haycock, 2001).

Clear and public standards for what students should learn at benchmark grade levels enhance teachers', administrators', and parents' understanding of the knowledge and skills students need to master. Kentucky was the first state to embrace standards-based reform. In 1991, the Kentucky State

Table 3.1

Socially Acceptable Behavior, Discriminatory Assumptions, and the Policies and Practices They Support

Socially Acceptable Behavior	Discriminatory Assumption	Restrictive or Demeaning Organizational Policy or Practice
Expressing the belief that academic success depends solely on the home environment	Schools or individual school employees cannot enhance student achievement and performance.	Failure of school or district to develop standards and learning goals for all Black and Hispanic students
Using negative labels to describe low-achieving and underachieving students	Black and Hispanic students are intellectually inferior to their White counterparts.	Use of tracking and ability grouping and the implementation of a low-level curriculum aligned with nonexistent jobs. A preponderance of vocational courses for Black and Hispanic youth that limit their performance on standardized tests
Deciding to treat all students the same	Youth who need more academic support and assistance should and will get it at home.	Failure of school or district to implement policies that provide extra help to students who need it—especially Blacks and Hispanics who are likely to be victims of low expectations or outreach in earlier grades
Allowing the "best teachers" to teach the "best students" in the "best schools"	Good teaching should not be "wasted" on failing students.	Allowing teachers with the weakest academic foundation to teach at pre-dominately Black and Hispanic schools
Encouraging Black and Hispanic youth to pursue athletics and entertainment as career choices	Blacks and Hispanics are more brawn than brain.	More funds are spent on gym equipment than academic equipment. School buildings are old and unkempt, although the physical education program may be strong. Educational advancement is de-emphasized
Providing more structure and discipline for Black and Hispanic youth	Black and Hispanic youth are more likely to not conform and misbehave, so stricter rules and consequences for misbehavior are required.	Development of school rules that stifle expression and creativity and punish youth for displaying cultural communicative and/or behavioral norms unique to their respective subcultures

Legislature released an ambitious set of learning goals and declared that all children would meet those goals. The state's success and progress has been clear and compelling—poor children in Kentucky are, in fact, learning in all subject areas.

More rigorous curriculum and coursework have a positive impact on the achievement of formerly low-achieving students and enhance the success of work-bound students as well. The work ethic and performance discipline students develop as a result of a more rigorous curriculum can help them develop persistence in future endeavors. Haycock (2001) found that the intensity and quality of instruction and high school coursework are the most important determinants of success in college—more important than class rank or scores on college admissions tests.

High-level teaching allows children to exceed at high levels. Some students, however, require more time and more instruction.

Extending instruction in ways that fit the community—before school, after school, on weekends, or in the summer—has been very successful for some states. The state of Maryland provides varied forms of assistance to students who are not on track so they can pass the state's new high school graduation test. The city of San Diego provides time—sometimes within the regular school day—by doubling, even tripling, instructional time devoted to literacy and mathematics for students who need it. San Diego also provides training for all teachers.

School officials should recognize the fact that if school rules or policy decisions unfairly penalize or exclude Black or Hispanic students, they reflect institutional racism or bias. During my travels over the years, I have seen some examples of school rules and policies that have had this impact. Those rules include the following:

- A school's policy stating that all school cheerleaders should have shoulder-length hair. This policy excluded many Black girls. Hopefully, policies such as this one no longer exist.

- School policy that disciplines girls for wearing colored stockings, big earrings, or cornrow hairstyles, which is likely to cause unfair treatment for Black and Hispanic girls.

- School policy that suspends Black youth for playing the dozens when White youth are not disciplined for culturally comparable forms of playful teasing.

Understanding Barrier-Breaking Policy

As school officials develop plans to eliminate tracking, ability grouping, and other discriminatory practices, policies, and procedures, they must make certain school personnel, community members, and students (especially those who are not Black or Hispanic) understand why these measures are being taken: to eliminate institutional racism and promote equality.

School officials who are responsible for developing strategies to implement local, state, or national legislation must also be aware of the perceived intent and the practical impact of certain legislation on Black and Hispanic youth. For example, the Children's Defense Fund, under the leadership of Marian Wright Edelman, has as its trademark the slogan, "Leave No Child Behind." When the No Child Left Behind bill became public law in 2002, many heralded it as a piece of legislation that could make certain that each and every educational system would, in fact, leave no child behind. School officials and legislators must make certain the law lives up to its title.

In my travels around the country, however, I have heard the consternation of numerous educators and school officials who, while they laud the spirit of the No Child Left Behind Act, question the ability of this law to fulfill its intent and live up to its title. Reg Weaver, president of the National Education Association, has called on Congress to "fix" this law because "it has wrong priorities and forces students into a one-size-fits-all mandate, creating more bureaucracy and paperwork." Weaver also notes that "every child is unique and each child learns in different ways. Great public schools must give individual attention to every child and help children learn the way they learn best" (Weaver, 2003). Weaver's frustration with this federal mandate that children be expected to learn and grow at the same rate is shared by many educators with whom I've spoken. Expecting every 10-year-old to start reading at the same level, on the same date, at the same time is tantamount to believing that every 10-year-old will also reach the same height and same weight on the same date at the same time. This is not going to happen!

However, given the significant spirit of this federal law, educators must work with federal and state legislators to make certain children receive the best possible public education. One administrator with whom I spoke expressed concern that teachers who had worked very hard in many poor, predominantly Black and Hispanic schools to realize significant achievement gains might still be penalized if those gains didn't meet federal standards—even if the gains were greater than achievement gains at schools that were already meeting government standards. This must not be allowed to happen, and the No Child Left Behind law must be monitored so that teachers, schools, and districts are rewarded for whatever progress they have made—even if that includes a "safe harbor" provision for schools that are making real progress but have not met their state's goals. In a paper presented by Kati Haycock and Ross Weiner for the National Center on Education and the Economy Forum, "Implementing the No Child Left Behind Act," the authors noted that "if any school or subgroup within a school does not meet the statewide performance targets, but the number of students below proficient is reduced by ten percent from the previous year, the school still makes 'adequate year progress'" (Haycock & Weiner, 2003).

The question on the minds of many administrators is this: "What happens if the number of students below proficient level is only reduced by 8 or 9%?" Certainly, the anxiety of educators and administrators who are striving to meet state and federal standards cannot be ignored. If poor schools that have made significant progress that is still less than the 10% standard are forced to receive less money, or worse, close their doors, many feel students will suffer. Vouchers given to private and religious schools are not the answer. Many Black and Hispanic students might still be unable to attend private schools (that can still pick and choose who they want to admit) with vouchers that pay less than 100% of the tuition. Since the vast majority of poor Black and Hispanic youth are likely to remain in public schools, every effort must be exerted to ensure that public schools are much more responsive to student needs. Government standards must not pose an institutional barrier but should allow the requisite breakthrough so that all students benefit.

Eliminating the Barriers

Rather than allow federal legislation to serve as a barrier to long-term student success, school districts must implement additional strategies to enhance Black and Hispanic student achievement and obtain further progress under federal guidelines. Educators must remember that all institutional barriers to student achievement can be eradicated. Those institutional barriers to student achievement are identified when we ask the following questions of school officials and leaders:

- Are all Black, Hispanic, and poor students given the same rights and opportunities to advance as their White counterparts?

- What training of adult employees has taken place in the school or district to examine racist beliefs and assumptions?

- Are schools being rewarded for academic progress?

- Have discriminatory assumptions fueled the development of district and school policies?

- Are underqualified teachers still teaching at mostly Black and Hispanic schools?

- What steps have been taken to make certain Black, Hispanic, and poor parents are aware of your district's standards for student achievement benchmarks at each grade level?

- Are you satisfied that neither institutional racism nor prejudicial school policies exist in your school or school district?

- What steps is your school or district taking to make certain that "no child is left behind"?

As you reflect on your answers to the questions above, commit yourself anew to the elimination of both the institutional barriers and the school-related obstacles that not only preclude student success, but also limit school effectiveness.

Chapter 4

School-Related Obstacles to Student Achievement

"Blessed is he who expects nothing, for he shall never be disappointed."

—Anonymous

In the previous chapter, the discussion of institutional barriers to student achievement focused on the need to eradicate institutional racism and discriminatory or demeaning school and district policy. Importantly, we need to ensure that policy and legislation do not impede long-term progress in schools where there have been some achievement gains for Black and Hispanic students. Many of these schools are still labeled as "failing," despite laudable gains.

The purpose of this chapter is to provide an understanding and analysis of those school-related obstacles that have been known to stymie, thwart, and in some cases prevent the achievement of Black and Hispanic students. (Strategies to eliminate these obstacles are detailed in subsequent chapters.) Some school-related obstacles to the achievement of Black and Hispanic students are as follows:

- Lack of pluralistic curricula

- Incongruent teaching and learning styles

- Academic tracking and ability grouping

- Test bias

- Negative labeling

Lack of Pluralistic Curricula

The call for a holistic and comprehensive change in curricula is not new. In a 1977 study, the National Endowment for the Humanities found that deficiencies in knowledge of history and literature were most pronounced among Black and Hispanic youth. Schools were found to be fostering "class bias and elitism" by failing to offer adequate instruction in history and literature to those youth most at risk (Cheyney, Fine, & Ravitch, 1987). This study concluded that when youth were denied their history, they were unlikely to realize their full potential.

As the Roman orator Cicero wrote, "to know nothing of what happened before you were born is to remain forever a child" (cited in Cheyney, Fine, & Ravitch, 1987). When Gay (1990) called for a total reconceptualization of our views of American history and culture and of the ways they are taught and learned, she emphasized that cultural pluralism must become an accepted canon of American education. Ravitch (2000) has concluded that schools must (emphasis added):

- Help *all* students gain reading skills and math skills.

- Help *all* students develop a good understanding of history, the sciences, literature, and a foreign language.

- Teach *all* students the importance of honesty, personal responsibility, intellectual curiosity and industry, kindness, empathy, and courage.

- Prepare students to have "versatile intelligence" that allows them to learn new tasks and take charge of their lives.

- Teach youth to use symbolic language and abstract ideas.

- Teach children about the culture and world in which they live and about the culture that existed long ago and far away.

The curriculum must emphasize positive aspects of Black and Hispanic life experiences, lifestyles, and social and behavioral norms. This need for a more pluralistic curriculum has spawned the implementation of African-centered (or Afrocentric) curricula in some urban school districts. The intent of the African-centered curriculum is to enhance the dignity, pride, self-respect, and motivation of Black youth by enhancing their understanding of their heritage and cultural differences.

Whether a school system chooses an African-centered curriculum or a curricular model rooted in multiculturalism, it must do more than teach history. The school program must also address the need for changes in teacher attitudes, teaching strategies, assessment procedures, value orientation, and the content of what is taught. It is important to seek pluralism in the curriculum through efforts to determine:

- What is being taught?

- Why it is being taught?

- Who is educating Black and Hispanic students?

- How is the instruction provided?

What Is Taught?

Ravitch (2000, p. 466) observes that the disciplines taught in school are uniquely valuable, both for individuals and for society. She writes:

- A society that does not teach science to the general public fosters the proliferation of irrational claims and antiscientific belief systems.

- A society that turns its back on the teaching of history encourages mass amnesia, leaving the public ignorant of the important events and ideas of the human past and eroding the civic intelligence needed for the future.

- A democratic society that fails to teach the younger generation its principles of self-government puts these principles at risk.

- A society that does not teach youngsters to appreciate the great works of literature and art permits a coarsening and degradation of its popular culture.

- A society that is racially and ethnically diverse requires, more than other societies, a conscious effort to build shared values and ideals among its citizenry.

- A society that tolerates anti-intellectualism in its schools can expect to have a dumbed-down culture that honors celebrity and sensation rather than knowledge and wisdom.

There are many who believe that current school curricula focus on imparting knowledge that is largely irrelevant to the survival of Black and Hispanic youth. In order to be more relevant and effective in enhancing shared values and ideals, curricula must be revised to foster an appreciation of all of the positive components of the students' racial or cultural group as well as the most accurate portrayal of history from the perspective of that particular racial or cultural group.

Irrelevant school curricula distort historical facts—such as Columbus "discovering" America—and portray racial and ethnic groups negatively—such as when Native Americans are portrayed as "savages." Many Black and Hispanic youth who have been taught the truth outside of school will see such historical distortions as propaganda and irrelevant to their futures because they view such information as attempts to brainwash them. Also irrelevant to Black and Hispanic students are curricula that focus on "tradition" instead of truth, such as with the slave revolts and the hypocrisy of slave-holding American presidents like Thomas Jefferson and George Washington (Wright, 2003).

Similarly, Black and Hispanic youth are more likely to question the motives of their educators and national leaders when they see attempts to distort the messages of revered Black leaders. For example, when Martin Luther King, Jr., spoke of his "dream" that his children be "judged by the content of their character and not the color of their skin," he was responding to the bias that had denied equal access and equal opportunity to racial minorities for centuries. When students of color (and White students, too) see these words taken out of context, such as to justify an end to affirmative action (as they were by President George W. Bush on January 15, 2003), they are also more likely to believe that they are receiving propaganda and not relevant knowledge.

A curriculum is relevant for Black and Hispanic youth when it shares factual information about history (especially *their* history) and current events. A curriculum is also relevant when it builds on the students' cultural and nonacademic strengths and teaches students how to use their respective strengths to realize legitimate, meaningful goals (see chapter 5).

Why Is It Being Taught?

Educators must make certain they are not just imparting the skills and knowledge needed by students simply to survive in society. Black and Hispanic students must be groomed and prepared for careers that will bring them professional gratification and financial security. It is important, therefore, that these students are not put in vocational/technical or low-level tracks that only prepare them for menial labor or dead-end jobs. Many argue that the unequal distribution of wealth, power, and privilege is (and historically has been) the reality of American capitalism—a system that produces educational and occupational losers (Hare, 1979). The unequal teaching of skills, grading, routing, and credentialing procedures of our educational system play a critical role in legitimizing structural inequality in the American social system.

The current resegregation of many schools has created unequal educational opportunities for many Black and Hispanic students. In their study, "Schools More Separate: Consequences of a Decade of Resegregation," Gary Orfield and Nora Gordon found that much of the progress for Black students since the 1960s was eliminated during the 1990s, which brought three Supreme Court decisions limiting desegregation remedies. Their data also show that Hispanics, the nation's largest minority, have become increasingly isolated for the last 30 years, with segregation surpassing that experienced by Blacks. The rapid growth of suburban minorities has not produced integrated schools.

Resegregation is contributing to a growing gap in quality between schools attended by White students and those attended by Blacks and Hispanics. Despite the growing diversity in the U.S. and the 245% growth in the Hispanic student population since 1970, desegregation is still occurring at an alarming rate (Orfield & Gordon, 2001). Orfield and Gordon note the irony of this development, considering the fact that desegregated schools both improve test scores and positively change the lives of all students. Students with the same test scores tend to be much more successful in college if they attended interracial high schools (Orfield & Gordon, 2001). Given this reality, the question "Education for what?" takes on additional significance. Many feel that Black and Hispanic students in segregated schools are less likely to be prepared for the high-tech jobs of the 21st Century.

Currently, the percentages of Black and Hispanic students in low tracks, special education, alternative schools, and vocational programs far surpass that of Whites, even though they are still the minority school population (Losen, Orfield, & Daniel, 2002).

In citing data from the Office for Civil Rights, U.S. Department of Education, Elementary and Secondary School Civil Rights Compliance Reports of 2000, Losen, Orfield, and Daniel (2002) found that Black children were 16% of the total school enrollment, but comprised 38% of students labeled educationally mentally retarded (EMR). When these students become convinced that they are not likely to receive the education, skills, and training necessary to succeed legitimately in a high-tech society, they are more likely to believe schools are preparing them for menial labor and a life of poverty. With this notion, Black and Hispanic youth often take whatever skills, ingenuity, creativity, and intelligence they think they have and seek success through illegitimate, illegal, and illicit means. We cannot tease youth with the accoutrements of success yet deny them legal means of achieving this success when we educate them only for low-paying careers.

Who Is Educating Black and Hispanic Students?

According to the National Center for Education Statistics (NCES), fewer Black and Hispanic individuals are seeking to become teachers (2001). More effort must be put into the recruitment of Black and Hispanic teachers, and male teachers in particular. The NCES estimates that the pool of Black or Hispanic male teachers is now below 5% (2001). The American Association of Colleges for Teacher Education found in 1999 that 74% of elementary and secondary teachers were female and 87% of them were White. Blacks comprise only 7% of public school teachers, while 46% of elementary and secondary public school students are minorities (Snyder, 1999).

Hare (2001) found that student sex, race, social class, and background affect the quality of student-teacher relationships, with teachers responding most favorably to students of the same sex, race, and social class as themselves. In many cases, teachers who are unable to embrace the diversity of their students resent teaching them and behave in ways that foster a loss of confidence and debilitating self-criticism in students (Hare, 2001). The importance of moving teachers beyond their prior beliefs or feelings about diverse students cannot be understated. Those teachers who are capable of embracing multiple teaching strategies, pluralistic classroom environments, and multicultural course materials will have a positive impact on the achievement of their Black and Hispanic students.

How Is the Instruction Provided?

How instruction is provided is central to understanding who learns. Instructional strategies and teaching styles must tap the full range of student potential. Students respond more favorably when learning is related to their reality. As a teacher, I understood that if I was going to *teach* my students, I first had to *reach* my students. Teachers must make every effort to show students they care about them as people first, then as students.

How we teach is, in some cases, more important than *what* we teach. Therefore, every effort must be made to make the teaching styles of educators more congruent with the learning styles of their students.

Incongruent Teaching and Learning Styles

Students who find their culture and learning styles reflected in both the substance and the organization of the instructional program are more likely to be motivated, less likely to be disruptive, and more likely to benefit from their learning experience. In her book, *Black Children: Their Roots, Culture, and Learning Styles,* Janice Hale-Benson (1986) suggests that formal education has not worked for many Black youth because it has not employed the teaching styles that correspond with students' learning styles. Benson observes that Black youth have barely mastered the norms of their own culture when they are confronted with teaching styles that are incompatible with their accepted learning patterns.

When this incongruity between teaching and learning styles exists, Black and Hispanic children become less motivated and more likely to question their self-worth. When Black and Hispanic youth find learning difficult, many often blame themselves and develop animosity toward the educational environment. Ravitch (2000) concludes that children benefit most from well-educated teachers who are eclectic in their methods and who are willing to use different strategies depending on what works best for which children.

Before teachers can understand and appreciate the learning styles preferred by students, it is important that they understand the role that culture plays in shaping student learning styles. Culture shapes a child's cognitive development, approach to academic tasks, and behavior in traditional academic settings (Hale-Benson, 1982). Cultural conflict can occur when children have not had experiences that provide them with the kind of information that is used and valued in school.

To reach all children, educators must expand their repertoire of instructional strategies to include the various approaches children use to learn. In writing about Black children's learning styles, Hale-Benson (1982) suggests that many Black youth employ people-oriented and field-dependent (or field-sensitive) approaches to learning rather than the analytical style favored in most school structures. However, the obvious must be stressed: All Black and Hispanic children do not use the same learning style.

People-Oriented Learning

People-oriented learning is part of the African heritage. Because many Black youth learn in their preschool years through extensive social interaction, some Black or poor youth may have more difficulty than White students in settings where learning takes place primarily through the use of educational hardware, technology, books, listening stations, learning centers, television, programmed instruction, learning kits, and other objects (Hale-Benson, 1982). Because of the differences in culture, some Black youth can benefit from intensive personal interaction with teachers who provide rapport, nonverbal support, and affection. If educational hardware is used, it must be interactional to achieve the best results with Black, Hispanic, and poor youth.

Field-Dependent Learning

Research also indicates that a high percentage of Black and Hispanic children are *field-dependent*. The field-dependent, or field-sensitive, learner tends to be aware of the social and personal relevance of the learning experience. It matters to these youngsters that the materials and concepts are related within their own experience and are neither abstract nor isolated (Hale-Benson, 1982). Field-dependent learners prefer student-centered, more personal environments. They prefer small-group activities and thrive when given opportunities to exchange information with peers.

Field-independent learners, on the other hand, are more interested in concepts for their own sake. These students function very successfully in self-structured learning, enjoy learning isolated information, and like to work in independent, teacher-centered, impersonal environments. Children who are field-dependent prefer to work together for the benefit of the group in an atmosphere where the pace of learning is set by the momentum of the group rather than by imposed time constraints. These youth find it difficult to function in field-independent environments, where achievement results are from individual and often competitive efforts.

Table 4.1 (page 74) presents a number of major differences between field-dependent and field-independent learners.

Table 4.1

Learning Preferences

Field-Independent Students	Field-Dependent Students
Field-independent students prefer: • Independent projects; working alone • Hypothesis-testing approaches • Solving problems • A focus on details, moving from specific to general (phonics, structured rules in spelling and math) • Clear grading criteria with specific feedback • A teacher-centered environment	Field-dependent students prefer: • Group projects, sharing, discussions • Personal examples, anecdotes, stories • Relating learning to their own experiences • A focus on the big picture, moving from the general to the specific (whole-word language experience, reasons for rules) • Praise, assurance, working to please others, frequent interaction with teachers • A student-centered environment

Adapted from Howard (1987). *Learning to persist, persisting to learn.* Washington, DC: Mid-Atlantic Equity Center.

Given what we know about the impact of learning styles on student performance, educators who are serious about enhancing the motivation and achievement of Black and Hispanic youth must be willing to use a variety of activities to stimulate interest and facilitate student growth. Howard's research on learning styles indicates that active learning is more effective for these students than passive drill and practice exercises (1987). Similarly, Black and Hispanic youth are likely to respond favorably to think-pair-share activities, lively group discussions, cooperative learning, group projects, and telling stories about personal experiences. Teachers must keep in mind that children remember more of what teachers do than what teachers say. Thus, efforts to involve children in simulated activities will enhance their abilities to retain information as well as their desire to learn more.

Teachers will also discover that many active learners also are encouraged when course content and classroom activities relate to something in the students' own life experiences. Of real significance, however, is the powerful impact of a teacher's genuine and sincere interest in the well-being of the student. Personal compliments, praise, enthusiasm, and even hugs, when appropriate, often work wonders in keeping Black and Hispanic youth interested and excited about learning. Murnane (1975) found that youth will feel more positive about their abilities and self-worth when teachers provide sincere and necessary support and encouragement.

Good (1981) summarized how teachers communicate negative expectations through the following behaviors toward perceived underachievers:

- Providing students with general, often insincere praise

- Providing them with less feedback

- Demanding less effort of them

- Interrupting them more often

- Seating them farther away from the teacher

- Paying less attention to them

- Calling on them less often

- Waiting less time for them to respond to questions

- Criticizing them more often

- Smiling at them less

Teachers can reverse the consequences of low expectations by avoiding these behaviors. Remember, students don't care what you know unless they know that you care.

Academic Tracking and Ability Grouping

As noted in chapter 3, tracking and ability grouping are not only more blatant forms of institutional racism, they are also the means by which Black and Hispanic students are denied equal educational opportunities (*Hobson v. Hansen*, 1967). Therefore, tracking has been outlawed in some jurisdictions, but has continued to be a presence and a problem in many other jurisdictions as noted in research described in this section. Importantly, the failure rate of many Black and Hispanic youth can be attributed in part to "between and within" classroom ability grouping, which fosters development of a caste system in school that allows for downward, but not upward, mobility (Rist, 1978).

Lawler found that when children are tracked they are deprived of the opportunity to develop the skills needed for success in the labor force. Moreover, Lawler found that Black youth respond to tracking by being truant or by withdrawing mentally and emotionally from the learning experience (1978).

The June 1989 report by the Carnegie Council on Adolescent Development, "Turning Points," found that 25% of 10- to 17-year-olds in the United States were extremely vulnerable to school failure. The report found that in practice tracking has proven to be one of the most divisive and damaging of school practices. In a more recent report by the

Carnegie Council (Jackson & Davis, 2000), the authors found that tracking reinforces inaccurate and ultimately damaging assumptions about intelligence. The report goes on to state:

> *Tracking students by perceived ability level or past performance is a clear manifestation of unequal expectations. . . . Tracking is easily the most formidable structural barrier to equitable learning opportunities and positive group relations, given that minority-group students are disproportionately represented in the lower tracks. Tracking determines which students will have the best and most varied learning opportunities, and it denies all students the opportunity for routine and frequent interaction with other students unlike themselves.* (p. 175)

Prior to the Carnegie Council reports, Oakes saw tracking as a major contributor to "mediocre schooling" and described the following consequences (1986):

- Initial differences among students are exaggerated rather than accommodated.

- School officials accept the achievement of a few at the expense of the majority.

- Barriers develop to prevent success for Blacks and Hispanics.

Tracking and ability grouping must be eradicated if we are to enhance the achievement of Black and Hispanic students. The practice is likely to send subliminal messages to Black and Hispanic youth that White and middle-class students are going to have opportunities for a greater range of knowledge and, therefore, opportunities for more lifelong success.

The extensive tracking of Black and Hispanic students in disproportionate numbers was first outlined in a 1980 study by Harnischfeger and Wiley. This study showed that 24.1% of the public school population was Black and Hispanic but only 13.8% of those students were in gifted and talented programs. The overrepresentation of Blacks and Hispanics in lower-ability groups, as well as in vocational and general tracks, was also well-documented in the same study. However, in the decades since 1980, there is evidence that there has been no change in the disproportionate overrepresentation of Blacks and Hispanics in special education or low-ability classes. In fact, the situation has worsened.

In their analysis of the overrepresentation of Blacks and Hispanics in special education, Harry and Anderson (1994) found that, according to the U.S. Department of Education Office for Civil Rights, although Blacks were 16% of the U.S. public school enrollment in 1999, they accounted for over 32% of special education placements and only 9% of gifted and talented placements. Harry and Anderson define "disproportionate" as plus or minus 10% of the percentage that would be expected on the basis of school-age population. If, they noted, Blacks accounted for 16% of the U.S. public school enrollment, then the special education enrollment should fall within a range of plus or minus 1.6% of the total enrollment. Hence, the percentage of special education placements falling outside of the range from 14.4% to 17.6% would be considered disproportionate (Harry & Anderson, 1994).

Some may argue that the disproportionate special education placement of Blacks and Hispanics does not reflect bias at all but rather the disproportionately high learning difficulties of these students and should be considered appropriate intervention. Yet Heller, Holtzman, and Messick (1982) found that opportunities for academic success are restricted and educational progress stymied when expectations and goals for students are lowered or inappropriate. In a 1994 critique of the process for determining placements, Harry and Anderson found that this disproportionate representation is likely to continue if special education or low-ability placement is based on instruction or assessment through testing. The perils of test bias are discussed in the next section.

Alternatives to Tracking and Ability Grouping

Instead of tracking and ability grouping, teachers should make effective use of heterogeneous grouping and cooperative learning strategies. There are five basic elements of heterogeneous grouping and cooperative learning (Hale-Benson, 1982):

1. *Mixed achievement and accomplishments*—Students with differing levels of academic accomplishment work together. Usually high-, middle-, and under-achieving students are put in cooperative learning groups.

2. *Positive interdependence*—Each member of the group understands that there will be mutual goals (goal interdependence); divisions of labor (task interdependence); division of materials, resources, or information among group members (resource interdependence); assignment of students to differing group roles (role interdependence) based on nonacademic or academic strengths; and joint rewards (reward interdependence).

3. *Face-to-face interaction*—The interaction between students, verbal interchange, and mutual support affects education outcomes.

4. *Individual accountability*—Students must provide appropriate support and assistance to one another so that the achievement of each student is maximized.

5. *Use of interpersonal and small group skills*—Teachers must first teach the social skills needed for collaboration so students are motivated to use their own social skills. Importantly, students must be given the time and procedures for analyzing how well their learning groups are functioning and the extent to which students are employing their social skills to help all group members achieve and maintain effective working relations within the group.

Cooperative learning does not mean that students will merely sit side-by-side at the same table and talk to each other while they do individual assignments. Nor does this approach mean that a group of students will put their names on an assignment that only one student has completed. If done correctly, the use of heterogeneous grouping and cooperative learning has the advantage of being more democratic. The content, teaching methods, classroom climate, and teacher-student interaction of heterogeneous classrooms often resemble average and upper track classes (Hale-Benson, 1982). Studies have found that providing a common learning experience to students with different backgrounds, interests, cultures, and plans for the future—in small groups—results in high achievement for students at all previous tracking levels (Parker & Parker, 1981).

Test Bias

Culturally biased tests should not be used for the placement of Black and Hispanic youth because they do not reflect the true ability of many students. The fairness of standardized tests for cultural and racial minorities was again questioned in 1994 by Gipps. Fairness is often challenged because many tests, such as the Stanford-Binet Intelligence Test, include items that assess moral opinions and other values that reflect social class bias rather than ability (Hilliard, 1976). In addition, Taylor (1987) found that many standard tests reflect communication-related biases such as those presented in Table 4.2 (page 82). Orfield (2001) found that when school districts raise standards for testing and graduation, more bias often results if there is inequality in student exposure to knowledge, teaching quality, and preparation.

IQ Testing

IQ tests are considered by many experts as one tool used to deny equal educational opportunities to Black and Hispanic youth. In his study of the impact of IQ testing on student placement, Asa Hilliard suggested that educators must find alternatives to IQ testing in order to identify giftedness in Black and Hispanic children (Hilliard, 1976). Indeed, the placement of Black and Hispanic students through the use of culturally biased standardized testing is seen by many as a cover for in-school resegregation (Harry & Anderson, 1994). In some states, the courts have addressed the issue of placement through testing and concluded that minorities should not be placed through the use of biased IQ testing and other instruments. The California Court Case of *Larry P. V. Wilson Riles* (1979) is one example.

In the Larry P. case, the San Francisco Unified School District was accused of discriminating against five Black children who had been placed in special education classes for the mentally retarded (EMR). At that time in San Francisco, 29% of the student enrollment was Black, while 66% of the EMR students were Black. In the state as a whole, 10% of the student

Table 4.2

Sources of Communication and Communication-Related Biases in Tests and Assessment Procedures

Situational Bias	Mismatches between examiner and examinee regarding the social rules of language. For example, sarcastic answers to obvious questions: Examiner—What time does the clock say? Examinee—Everybody knows clocks don't talk.
Directions Bias	Test directions involve linguistic complexities unfamiliar to the examinee. For example: "None of the following are true except..." is incorrectly interpreted as "All of the following are true except..."
Value Bias	Examinee is required to exhibit a particular moral or ethical preference. For example: "One who is dishonest is... a. An offender b. A politician c. An ambassador d. An officer"
Linguistic Bias	Test presumes that examinee is competent in Standard English. For example: "Which sentence is grammatically incorrect? a. They saw Rose. b. You done it wrong. c. My brother has never eaten. d. Don't use too much."
Format Bias	Test procedures or requirements are inconsistent with examinee's cognitive and/or learning style. For example: "Select the best answer to the following..."
Cultural Misinterpretations	Examiner erroneously interprets cultural practices of examinee. For example, a child who exhibits silence as a natural reaction to an unfamiliar adult examiner is diagnosed as nonverbal, or a child who does not respond quickly to test items is deemed unknowledgeable.

Adapted from Taylor (1987). *Cross-cultural communication: An essential dimension of effective education* (pp. 26–27). Washington, DC: Mid-Atlantic Equity Center.

body was Black, while 25% of the EMR students were Black. The plaintiffs claimed that the use of biased IQ tests for placement purposes constituted a violation of the 14th Amendment rights for these students. Although courts in Indiana and other states have also concluded that minorities should not be placed through the use of biased IQ tests, the practice continues, and the disproportionate representation of Blacks and Hispanics is unabated.

Alienation and Psychological Withdrawal

Another consequence of test bias is the alienation and physical or psychological withdrawal of underachieving students from the learning process due to their inability to master enough mainstream culture to perform well on culturally biased exams. The inability of some underachieving Black and Hispanic youth to master mainstream White culture has caused some educators to view cultural differences in their Black and Hispanic students as indicators of deficiencies (Hilliard, 1976). Hale-Benson (1982) found that biased tests have figured prominently in the destruction of self-concept and the denial of educational opportunity.

Thus, test bias ultimately causes Black and Hispanic students to feel more alienation, more isolation, and less motivation. Many simply stop trying to achieve academically. Subsequently, they withdraw from the learning process and seek other means of "achieving" in the classroom—even if it means being disruptive. Just as the data reveal the disproportionate representation of Black and Hispanic students in low-ability tracks and special education classes, the data also show that Black males receive corporal punishment in schools at close to four times the rate of Whites and are suspended at almost three times the rate (U.S. Department of Education, Office for Civil Rights, 1998).

Test bias is also likely to reinforce negative attitudes toward the school from parents who recognize and appreciate the social skills of their children and who themselves felt victimized by culturally biased tests during their school years. While much more will be said in chapter 8 about the fragile relationship between parents and educators, it should be noted here that if parents of Black and Hispanic youth feel that schools were unfair when they were students, schools are likely to appear to be even more unfair to their children. In the post-desegregation era, more Black and Hispanic parents are concerned with the alienation of their children from the learning process.

Many Black and Hispanic parents do understand the power of the self-fulfilling prophecy. I have counseled parents who have noted that the placement of their children in special education classes and the concomitant effects of that placement over a period of time were sufficient to cause the student to assume the characteristics of the disability, even though the placement was based on subjective teacher analysis, misdiagnosis, or tests that did not accurately measure ability or potential. Some Black and Hispanic youth who are labeled BD (Behavioral Disordered) and placed in EMR classes are simply showing behavior unique to their culture. Kunjufu (1985) found that the aggressive verbal "volleying" of Black boys is often interpreted as hostile and threatening by the female culture of the school. Once labeled a "behavior problem," the student then becomes one.

Test bias can also lower the expectations of teachers who fail to understand that lower scores of some Black and Hispanic youth are more an indication of cultural conflict than low intelligence. Gilbert and Gay (1985) found that Black students who are misdiagnosed and misplaced have difficulty in the regular classroom because the classroom environment is not set up to meet the needs of this culturally diverse population. Harry and Anderson (1994) concluded that cultural preferences for both physical and verbal behavior have a powerful influence on teachers' perceptions, which are the source of the initial referral of children for special education evaluation. Those children who are less malleable to conformity are often seen as the most deficient academically. The cultural conflict felt by many Black and Hispanic students causes some to develop an "oppositional identity" where being smart is the opposite of being cool, and their test scores—like other measures of academic performance—decline (Tatum, 1997).

Bias-Free Tests

In 1978, during a study of IQ heredity and racism, Lawler concluded that it was nearly impossible to develop a "culture free" test because no test could possibly incorporate materials and skills common to all cultures. However, the SOMPA Test (System of Multicultural Pluralistic Assessment) is a testing instrument that is non-biased toward all ethnic groups. It is described in Table 4.3 (page 86). Educators can also enhance student performance on tests that accurately measure ability, progress, and potential (as opposed to an understanding of White culture). Criterion-referenced tests have grown in popularity because they are based on what has actually been taught in school. These tests are unlikely to be timed and allow students to show mastery of specific materials.

Teachers can also evaluate students with assessment instruments more likely to measure true ability. These include oral exams (especially when a child has shown difficulty in taking written tests), class projects, group assignments, and other simulated materials designed to provide more accurate indications of understanding and skill mastery.

Table 4.3

System of Multicultural Pluralistic Assessment

Purpose	Designed to assess the educational needs of children in a culturally nondiscriminatory manner
Population	Ages 5 to 11
Score	Provides assessment in three areas: medical, social systems, and pluralistic systems
Time	4 to 5 hours
Authors	Jane Mercer and June Lewis; published by The Psychological Corporation
Description	The System of Multicultural Pluralistic Assessment (SOMPA) was designed to be responsive to the mandates of PL 94/142; that is, to assess the educational needs of children ages 5 to 11 years of age in a racially and culturally nondiscriminatory manner. Its construction and recommended usage are derived from an explicit ideological view as to what American society should be like (i.e., culturally pluralistic). Thus, unlike most psychometric devices, the SOMPA authors openly express their ideological assumptions (intelligence and learning potential are distributed equally among all ethnic and racial groups) and express their hopes that its use will promote cultural pluralism.
Scoring	The medical perspective focuses on the presence or absence of organic pathology. Six measures are employed: Physical Dexterity Tasks (sensory motor coordination), The Bender Visual Motor Gestalt Test

(continued)

Table 4.3 (continued)

System of Multicultural Pluralistic Assessment

	(perceptual and neurological factors), The HealthHistory Inventories, Weight by Height Norms (nutritional or developmental problems), Vision (the Snellen Test), and Auditory Acuity (national norms).
	The social systems perspective deals with how the child's behavior conforms to the social norms of the various social groups in which the child participates. These instruments are used: the Adaptive Behavior Inventory for Children (ABIC) and the Wechsler Intelligence Scale for Children—Revised (WISC-R)
	The third perspective, the pluralistic model, is unique to the SOMPA. Its procedures are designed to yield an index of the child's intelligence or Estimated Learning Potential through a "corrected" WISC-R score that is based on a comparison of how well the child performs on that test with other children who have had similar learning opportunities (i.e., from a similar sociocultural background).
Reliability and Validity	The reliability and validity for the separate measures comprising the SOMPA appear to be satisfactory.
Norms	SOMPA measures were standardized on 2,100 California children ranging in age from 5 to 11. The measures comprising the SOMPA were individually standardized upon creation.

Source: Mercer, J., & Lewis, J. (1979). *System of Multicultural Pluralistic Assessment (SOMPA): Technical manual.* San Antonio, TX: Psychological Corporation.

Instructional strategies that will also enhance the learning and understanding of Black and Hispanic youth must be implemented. Intradistrict disparities in school funding, teaching time, instruction, and school curricula must be addressed if test bias is to be eradicated. Almost all students can achieve at high levels if they are taught at high levels. Many poor, Black, and Hispanic students require more time and more instruction (Haycock, 2003).

Negative Labeling

While it is understood that schools and educators must help students overcome their academic deficiencies, too much emphasis is often placed on the use of negative labels to describe the student. Given what educators already know about the power of self-fulfilling prophecy (such as, students tend to respond to our expectations and opinions of them), the use of negative labels to describe students must not continue.

In 1996, I had the opportunity to carefully review teachers' comments in the cumulative folders of Black and Hispanic female students labeled "troublemakers" in a middle school in Washington, DC. I discovered the following descriptors: "too talkative," "disrespectful," "too grown," "sassy," "lacks social skills," "obnoxious," "hardened," and "hostile." Although I was not surprised by the use of such negative labels, I was nonetheless disappointed. When teachers focus only on negative attributes of students, they are less likely to help students develop the confidence they need to overcome academic and behavioral weaknesses. Many Black, Hispanic, and poor students who have little or no confidence will believe the worst things they hear about themselves.

Rather than reinforce inappropriate behavior with "negative" labels, teachers can substitute denigrating labels with language that is more positive in describing the student's behavior or character weakness. The goal should not be to judge unfairly or demean a student, but to help that student develop into a positive, productive adult. The following are examples of how the previously mentioned "negative" labels can be replaced with more positive descriptors.

A student who is:

Too talkative	Is expressive, loquacious, a future motivational speaker
Disrespectful	Shows no shortage of self pride
Too grown	Exhibits maturity and is self-assured
Sassy	Has a quick wit and a sharp tongue
Lacks social skills	Is introverted, quiet
Obnoxious	Is prone to excesses in innocent irritation
Hardened	Is an old soul, has seen a lot of life's sordid side
Hostile	Expresses feelings of being misunderstood

When the focus is on facilitating student behavioral change and positive character development, teachers must seek creative ways to enlist the support of other caring adult *Merchants of Hope*. The use of negative labels may discourage other adults from positive intervention. However, when adults (especially teachers, school officials, parents, and mentors) can build on student nonacademic strengths and turn negative character flaws into opportunities for positive growth, they will have overcome a major obstacle to student growth and achievement.

It should also be noted that many students are mislabeled as ADHD—they are thought to have Attention Deficit Hyperactivity Disorder. Such mislabeling is another major obstacle to student achievement.

ADHD is a syndrome characterized by problems with attention span, impulse control, and sometimes hyperactivity (Mendler, 1992). According to the American Psychiatric Association's DSM II-R, there are 14 symptoms associated with ADHD. A child must display at least eight of these symptoms over the course of a 6-month period before an accurate diagnosis can be made:

1. Fidgets, squirms, or seems restless

2. Has difficulty remaining seated

3. Is easily distracted

4. Has difficulty waiting his or her turn

5. Blurts out answers

6. Has difficulty following instructions

7. Has difficulty sustaining attention

8. Shifts from one uncompleted task to the next

9. Has difficulty playing quietly

10. Talks excessively

11. Interrupts others

12. Does not seem to listen

13. Often loses things necessary for tasks

14. Frequently engages in dangerous actions

Before my son, Kashif, was diagnosed accurately for the ADHD syndrome, he was thought to be a "discipline problem." Many other students may be similarly mislabeled negatively as behavioral problems when they may have neurological problems requiring medical intervention, at worst, and a change in the learning environment and teacher strategies at best. Quite often, students who have been labeled negatively or who are mislabeled as ADHD may lose their motivation to learn. The tips on "Motivating the Unmotivated," included in chapter 5 will help educators develop appropriate strategies to educate those frustrated learners who need more assistance.

Focusing Our Efforts

School improvement efforts must focus on removing obstacles to student achievement that are, in fact, a creation of school practices and policy. Requisite change can and must occur. School boards and administrators can certainly develop more pluralistic curricula. Teachers can be trained to develop teaching styles that are more congruent with the learning styles of their students. Academic tracking and ability grouping can be replaced with heterogeneous grouping and cooperative learning. Bias-free exams can be developed and implemented and the self-fulfilling consequences of negative labeling can be abated through the practice of labeling students more positively.

If school administrators and school boards can make these necessary improvements, students in entire districts will benefit. However, in the absence of comprehensive district reform, dedicated teachers can make a positive difference. The removal of these obstacles in the classroom will surely help. More information on motivating unmotivated students is shared in the following chapter.

Chapter 5

Motivating the Unmotivated

All children want to learn and can learn. . . .

—Collins, Tamarkin, and Haley, 1990

The previous chapters provide insight into and information for facilitating changes in the attitudes, behaviors, and structure of our schools. This chapter goes a step further. It examines the lack of motivation—real and perceived—among Black and Hispanic students. Much has been said about this lack of motivation. It is unfortunate, but many youths who exhibit low motivation may fail to reach their full potential not because they do not want to learn, but because it is impossible for them to learn. Many are put in situations in which they cannot learn, or are responding to the behavior and low expectations of those around them. This chapter should excite teachers about the role they can play in motivating Black and Hispanic children.

Black and Hispanic youth will respond positively to a learning environment conducive to school success. When teachers allow the restraints of low expectations, inappropriate curriculum, incongruent teaching styles, ability grouping, and test bias to determine what they do and how they motivate students, they can be sure of at least one thing: neither teacher nor student will be successful. When teachers are not imaginative or inspired, they are less likely to show the creativity and excitement in the classroom that generate excitement in their learners. As schools compete for children's time and attention with television, movies, mass media, and the Internet, they must reassert their primary responsibility for the development of young people's intelligence and character.

I am not suggesting that teachers lack the desire to teach—quite the contrary. As I have said before, most teachers are especially well-intentioned and sincere. Many are actually frustrated, however, by a perceived inability to reach Black and Hispanic youth. It is this frustration that I would like to address by considering how we can keep children excited about learning and educate them for the real world.

Keeping Children Excited About Learning

Recent data on dropout rates underscore the need for more efforts to keep children excited about education and their chances for lifelong success. According to Bonsteel (2001), "data from the U.S. Department of Education make it clear that U.S. high school graduation [rates have] fallen precipitously since 1993. [By 1999] one out of every four U.S. high school students [dropped] out of school before graduation." However, these data do not include the vast numbers of students who are "pushed out" of school when they turn 16. Students are pushed out for several reasons. First, they may be frequently absent because of out-of-school suspensions or truancy (which often stems from the unwelcome climate of the school). Second, they may have been retained so often that they are still in middle or junior high school by the time they turn 16; they are in effect forced out or pushed out of school by school officials who often show no desire to keep them or to enhance their academic achievement. Students who are expelled from school without due process are also pushed out by educators and administrators who would rather not expend the necessary time or energy educating these students.

When figures for youth who never make it to high school because they have been pushed out are included, the dropout rates for Black and Hispanic students 16 and over is close to 50% in some urban cities (Bonsteel, 2001). Another perspective on the problem is provided in the same report that noted that one of four U.S. high school students had dropped out of school by 1999. A table based on U.S. census data provides a sobering look at how the problem continues as youth of high school age become young adults. The percentage of youth ages 18–24 who had completed high school (with a diploma, the GED, or another form) was 8.8% for White youth, 16.5% for Black youth, and 36.6% for Hispanic youth (Kaufman, Kwon, Klein, & Chapman, 2000). Only youth who were no longer in high school were included in these data. In other words, of youth 18–24 no longer in high school, 1 of 6 Black and 1 of 3 Hispanic youth had not completed high school.

Whether or not you are in a school district with a relatively high dropout rate or no dropout rate at all, remember that many students may remain in school physically although they have already dropped out mentally and emotionally. The bottom line is the same, though; they have become alienated from the learning process. Therefore, adults' efforts to keep children in school should also focus on developing and strengthening the students' desire to be in school; however, keeping students in school should never be the sole objective. Efforts must also be made to help them learn while in school.

But schools must do more than teach children how to learn and how to look things up—they must prepare youth for the real world. Therefore, they must teach children what knowledge has the most value, how to organize what they know, how to understand the relationship between past and present, how to tell the difference between accurate information and propaganda, and how to turn information into understanding (Ravitch, 2000). When students feel that schools are preparing them for the real world, they tend to be more excited about learning.

Educating Students for the Real World

Educators must remember that as Black and Hispanic students move from elementary to middle schools and through high school, preparation for the real world must address questions minority youth will have about their racial and cultural identity and how society will respond to them because of their race and culture. Tatum (1997) notes that adolescents of color are more likely to be actively engaged in exploration of their racial or ethnic identity than White adolescents because of the racial messages they receive from White society.

Children of color must believe that academic achievement will improve their status, benefits, and general prosperity. Some teachers may be unable to give hope to children of color because they do not really believe these children *can* succeed academically. As a result, many Black and Hispanic youth think of themselves as trapped in a society with limited or nonexistent opportunities for significant and legitimate upward mobility. The current existence of a growing "underclass" of Black and Hispanic youth is an indication that these youth see an absence of opportunity for significant change in income, social roles, and social class status. Consequently, they stop seeking academic success or legitimate work in mainstream society after leaving school and opt instead for survival through more deviant systems—robbery, burglary, selling drugs, larceny, and murder (Glasgow, 1980).

However, the tremendous growth of young "antisocial" Blacks who have made millions in the hip-hop culture, entertainment industry, and professional sports is proof that many alienated youth who are still driven by ambition will find alternate routes to success within their own cultures or through their own culturally acceptable means—without sacrificing their racial identity. The tragedy is that too many young Black and Hispanic youth believe they can *only* be legally successful and prosperous through entertainment or sports.

Thus, it is imperative that educators and concerned adults take the necessary steps to harness the strengths of children of color and provide them with the means for true, legal success in our mainstream society. When motivated, Black and Hispanic students can be enthusiastic learners.

School officials can use many strategies to rekindle the excitement and joy of learning among Black, Hispanic, and poor students. I say "rekindle" because most kindergarteners are excited about starting school, but these students lose their passion and motivation for learning somewhere along their educational journey.

Ten Tips for Teaching Terrific Children

The following strategies will help educators rekindle student motivation and academic success and, in the process, help them to derive greater gratification from working with children:

1. Develop strong bonds with diverse students.

2. Identify and build on the strengths of all students.

3. Help students overcome their fear of failure.

4. Help students overcome their rejection of success.

5. Set short- and long-term goals with and for your students.

6. Develop appropriate teaching styles that are more congruent with the learning style preferences of Black and Hispanic students.

7. Use homework and television to your advantage.

8. Communicate to ensure your real intentions are understood.

9. Establish a good school and classroom climate where children receive the ongoing support and encouragement they need to succeed.

10. Strengthen relations between the home and school.

Develop Strong Bonds With Diverse Students

Any teacher who really loves children can motivate them. However, that love must be unconditional. In too many instances, a teacher's love and appreciation of a student are *condition subsequent*, that is, the result of certain behavior and abilities in students. Instead, the teacher's love and appreciation should be *condition precedent*. A teacher's love should encourage favorable behavior from and enhance the abilities of students. When a student detects teacher detachment, disinterest, or disrespect, social and personal bonds become weakened.

In their research on the causes of delinquency, Fagan and Jones (1984) determined that it is the weakening of personal and social bonds with adults that leads to negative peer influences. Schools must provide strong external bonds through efforts to improve achievement, involve youth in activities perceived as important, and enhance students' belief in their own abilities and self-determination.

I have already discussed some school-related factors that alienate Black and Hispanic youth. However, even when there are institutional barriers (lack of a pluralistic curriculum, use of ability grouping and tracking, test bias), teachers can still motivate and encourage individual students through the power of personal and academic relations. According to Burnette (1999), these relationships are the most influential. Certain behaviors and instructional strategies nurture these relationships by enabling better teacher-student bonding (Burnette, 1999).

The power of educator-student relationships that are characterized by mutual trust cannot be understated. Strong bonds develop when teachers show respect for the student and his or her culture, life experiences, and unique learning style. Burnette (1999) found teachers most effective when they enthusiastically acknowledged students' individual and cultural differences and identified those differences in the most positive way. Interviews with some Black high school students who presented behavior challenges for staff revealed that they wanted their teachers to discover what their lives were like outside of school and that they wanted an opportunity to participate in the school's reward systems (Burnette, 1999).

Teachers must also see themselves as learners. Through a spirit of mutual inquiry, they can build strong bonds with students that foster support and augment student achievement and motivation. Once mutual trust is established, the teacher can involve the student in a learning process that takes into account the needs of both student and teacher, as well as the needs of the school (or system), and the needs of society in general. Even when it appears that these needs are in conflict, they are not necessarily at odds.

For example, a student may speak in a non-standard English dialect. The student may be unaware of the need for him to be able to speak Standard English. The teacher and the school, however, share a need for that child to be able to speak Standard English. Society has a commensurate need for leaders and laborers who are skilled in standard forms of communication. The teacher can help children understand that Standard English is required for them to achieve legitimate economic success in this country. At the same time, the teacher should show that the child's previously learned language skills also are valued and have a place in society. In casual conversation, students may choose to speak in a dialect or another language, be it Black English or Spanish. Both are legitimate forms of expression.

The needs of the teacher, the school, the student, and society can all be met through instruction that respects student differences in language and culture. An excited, understanding, and caring teacher can bond with a student, regardless of the student's background, language, race, or culture. As Black and Hispanic youth grow older, they become more aware of the institutional racism and the perception of them that their racially diverse teachers (and other adults) are likely to have. As these students internalize who they are and what it means to be Black or Hispanic in a White-dominated society, they seek the support of other students and adults who understand their many encounters with racism. Quite often, the so-called "self-segregation" of many Black and Hispanic students during lunchtime or at school functions is a direct result of the need for support these students have and their desire to spend time with those who understand their pain and their perspective (Tatum, 1997).

To ease the feelings of isolation many Black and Hispanic students have—especially when they are in desegregated schools—educators must take requisite steps to remove visible signs of institutional racism, such as a preponderance of Blacks and Hispanics in special education or lower track classes. Other visible signs of institutional racism, as discussed in chapter 3, are policies that clearly target racial groups.

Teachers must take more time to talk to diverse students and communicate positive feelings and unconditional support. In the classroom, teachers can use activities, plays, poems, and stories that favorably reflect many aspects of Black and Hispanic culture. Also, for older students, appropriate and inappropriate uses of cultural language and experiences with racism can also be topics for classroom discussion.

Identify and Build on the Strengths of All Students

In many of our schools, too much emphasis is placed on identifying student disabilities and deficiencies. Once deficiencies are identified, many educators spend an inordinate amount of time reminding both the student and the parent that those deficiencies exist. If students are allowed to believe that significant adults in their lives, such as teachers and parents, see them as incompetent and inferior, they are likely to see themselves in much the same way. Their destiny in life often is determined by how they see themselves in their formative years. Similarly, students with real learning disabilities are often seen in the most negative light.

While some Black and Hispanic youth may have legitimate learning disabilities, those disabilities should not obscure the fact that *all* students have unique strengths, or nonacademic gifts and talents, that should be used to build academic confidence.

I have counseled parents of many Black and Hispanic students who are dyslexic. A reading disorder, dyslexia is either *developmental* or *acquired.* Youth who struggle with dyslexia are often frustrated learners. Many seek success through deviant means or disruptive classroom behavior when they feel teachers and other students are likely to ridicule or tease them for their reading difficulties. It is more imperative than ever that the nonacademic strengths of these students be identified and exalted.

My son, Kashif, had some success in overcoming the visual-spatial difficulties unique with surface and phonological dyslexia. However, it was only after the recommendation of my friend and colleague, Dr. Marie Carbo, president of the Carbo Reading Style Institute of Syosset, New York, that I discovered the remedy that saved Kashif. Dr. Carbo's extensive research found that the use of colored transparency sheets could abate the visual-spatial difficulties of dyslexia that afflicted Kashif (Carbo, 1996).

My son also has auditory deficit disorder. It takes him a few seconds longer to process words and sounds. In discussions I've had around the country with parents and teachers, I've discovered that many Black and Hispanic youth who have auditory deficit disorder go through school labeled unfairly before being diagnosed in their later years. Children with auditory deficit disorder are often the ones who ask for repetition of directions, instructions, and so forth. They are also likely to receive poor grades in conduct because teachers feel they "don't listen" and "don't follow directions." They

Dyslexia: A Common Problem

Developmental dyslexia is caused by biological anomalies (which are usually genetic) in the brain at various levels from prenatal through childhood development. *Acquired dyslexia,* however, is caused by brain trauma that may occur during prenatal months or later and has the same behavioral characteristics of developmental dyslexia.

There are four subgroups for dyslexia:

1. Surface: A person can read words phonetically but has problems with the whole word recognition (such as, yacht ➜ yachted).

2. Phonological: A person can read words by using whole word method but has difficulty sounding out words that are new; or the person has letter-to-sound decoding problems.

3. Spelling: A person can read individual letters that lead to reading words if given enough time but has problems recognizing the word as a whole and phonetically (such as, man ➜ hen).

4. Direct: A person can read aloud without comprehension.

All children who are dyslexic do not show the same symptoms. There are three categories of dyslexia.

1. Visual-spatial difficulties: Dyslexia occurs when children (or adults) cannot recognize groups of letters. They may tend to guess words by shape and not by context. People with this form of dyslexia may also confuse reversible letters, transposing letters in syllables and syllables in words and words in phrases. They have trouble reproducing letters in writing and may confuse letter, syllable, and word order. They may also read words backwards. Sometimes, letters actually seem to be moving.

2. Speech/sound difficulties: Dyslexia occurs when children (or adults) have problems understanding spoken language. Difficulty arises in breaking words into syllables and in forming sentences.

3. Correlating differences: Dyslexia occurs when persons are unable to find the appropriate speech sounds for individual letters or sounds in writing.

are also likely to be labeled "hard-headed"—even by their own parents who may not realize a disability is present.

Learning disabilities may be genetic. If a teacher discovers there have been other family members with learning disabilities, it might be wise to have children who appear to be struggling tested as well. When I learned as much as possible about Kashif's biological mother, I discovered that both of her other children were special learners like Kashif, who I adopted when he was 16 months old.

Building confidence. Although learning disabilities and learning difficulties can sap student confidence, they must never be allowed to destroy a student's hope. It becomes extremely important for teachers to implement strategies that can build confidence. The best way to build the confidence children need to overcome academic shortcomings is to build students' nonacademic strengths. When teachers identify students' nonacademic gifts, they let students know they see the students as competent and capable. Bonding becomes much easier. Also, teachers are able to provide opportunities for disabled students to experience success in *something* when they know their strengths, capabilities, and competencies.

Teachers and all adults who work with and around children (parents, too!) must remember that all children have nonacademic gifts and talents. *Every* teacher should put three adjectives that describe three nonacademic strengths next to the name of every child in the roll book. During the course of the instructional program, teachers can then provide students with opportunities to display their nonacademic strengths and talents in ways that enhance academic learning. For example, students can use dramatic or musical skills in role playing or debating (Kuykendall, 1989).

In teaching parts of speech to Black and Hispanic students in Newark public schools, I quickly discovered the strengths of my dramatic and assertive students. I had my more dramatic students perform skits where each person was given a specific role to play. Someone was a noun and someone else was an adjective who had to find the noun he was to describe. A variation of this activity was to tell the adverb to stand next to the noun, rather than the verb; commas to put themselves in the wrong sequence; and participles to dangle. The rest of the class had fun specifying where each part (person) was supposed to be. My students learned parts of speech through my efforts to teach to their strengths.

Once I identified individual nonacademic strengths in my students, I helped them to set goals for themselves based on those strengths. One of my former students, a 15-year-old seventh grader called "Lyin' Louis" by other teachers, became a personal project for me when he wound up in my English class and homeroom. By letting Louis know that I saw in him a "genius," I got him to believe in his own ability to be a legitimate success as an adult. Before I met him, Louis was headed down life's low road. With an incarcerated father and uncle, an unemployed mother, and a depressed adult home community, he received little motivation, inspiration, or encouragement and had no role models other than the hustlers who awed and inspired Louis's many friends. I discussed with Louis the lifestyle he *could* have if he were to use his lightning-fast wit, charm, guile, cunning, intuition, and people skills to make it as a politician, an entrepreneur (as the neighborhood's "pharmaceutical rep," he knew a little bit about running a "business"), or an attorney.

For the 2 years I was in his life, I reminded Louis incessantly of what he *could* be. Louis *did* graduate from high school at the age of 20 and, after spending four years at a community college, went on to become a lawyer. In my travels around the world, I've heard many stories of positive results that come when adults take time to identify and build on nonacademic strengths—even when those "strengths" manifest in negative behavior, such as lying, sneaking, cheating, arrogance, or carelessness.

Adults can handle some forms of negative behavior in positive ways. The following strategies should help educators build on the nonacademic strengths of their students that they find to be the most disturbing:

- A child who *lies* must be reminded that he has been blessed with the power of knowing intuitively what to say (and make people believe it).

- A child who *sneaks* can be reminded that her daring and courage may serve her very well one day but *only* if she uses this strength wisely.

- A child who *cheats* should be reminded of his endearing ambition and his determination. He should know these qualities need not lead to negative behavior but should only strengthen his resolve to be better prepared.

- A child who displays *arrogance* should be reminded that the self-confidence she has in abundance should make her more willing to help others feel as good. This means, of course, that the child should be encouraged and assisted in developing humility and a spirit of thanksgiving.

- A child who is *careless* must be reminded that some of history's most revered geniuses have been, like him or her, also focused so much on the big picture that they gave scant attention to detail and often overlooked small things and misjudged their surroundings—a kind of carelessness.

Teachers should habitually call their students by descriptive titles that reflect not only the child's nonacademic strengths but also goals that can be pursued because of their strengths. For example, students can be called "Attorney Andy," "Dr. Smith," "Professor Williams," "General José," or "Fireman Freddy" to name a few.

When a teacher builds on student strengths, it is easier to help that student to clarify his own aspirations for improved behavior and to diagnose the gaps between his aspirations and his present level of performance. The teacher then presents himself as a person who appreciates the real worth, feelings, and ideas of that student. The word "teacher" has its roots in the Latin word *educo* meaning to lead or to draw out. Good teachers can bring out the best in every student by acknowledging and strengthening individual and cultural strengths rather than causing self-doubt through a preoccupation with students' weaknesses.

Acknowledge family and cultural strengths through class discussions or writing activities in which students reflect upon family and personal experiences that have facilitated their growth, evoked special feelings, or taught them a sense of responsibility. Teachers also can use activities that emphasize those things that make the heritage of a particular student special or allow students to engage in dramatic readings or role plays where they can dramatize some of the cultural values and behaviors of all races. Poems by Langston Hughes, Paul Laurence Dunbar, Gwendolyn Brooks, Rita Dove, and other Black poets would provide such opportunities for Black youth. Hispanic American poets include Julia Alvarez, Sandra

Cisneros, Alberto Ríos, and Gary Soto. Black and Hispanic students can be asked to prepare and perform skits or role plays to show pride in their culture, their historical figures, or holidays, such as Kwanzaa or Cinco de Mayo.

In building on the strengths students bring to school, teachers can bring out their hidden potential, thereby strengthening both their social and academic self-images. By building confidence, teachers will be able to reduce the fear of failure that causes many Black and Hispanic students to give up before they realize their full potential.

Help Students Overcome Their Fear of Failure

All of us have, at some point in our lives, refrained from doing something because we felt we would not succeed. Fear of failure is real. If a child has experienced failure before, he or she does not want to experience it again. A person with a low self-image is likely to use fear of failure as an excuse for giving up or avoiding effort altogether. When individuals have strong self-images, fear of failure can be motivational.

Teachers can help students overcome their fear of failure by first letting every child know that he or she will succeed in the learning environment. Teachers must encourage students to see all failure as a learning experience. The feeling of confidence that comes from encouragement will make it easier for students to use failure constructively and to persist. Persistence is a learned behavior (Howard, 1987). Teachers will be hard pressed to teach persistence unless they have it themselves.

Teachers can also use examples of famous persons who achieved greatness because they persisted and persevered when dealing with setbacks. Abraham Lincoln is such an example. He never considered himself a failure—even though he had numerous setbacks (Donald, 1995). Table 5.1 (page 110) shares many of Lincoln's setbacks and successes. Unless children are taught to persist in academic endeavors, their setbacks may cause them to develop fear of academic failure. They must know that persistence will bring about success in most situations.

Many children who fear academic failure must also be reminded that they have already overcome fear of failure in social and recreational activities. Teachers can remind these children of the experience they had in learning to ride a bike, for example. Although every bike rider has fallen down, children who learned to ride bikes can appreciate the fact that they learned to ride because they refused to give up. Similarly, each child can ride the bike called "reading," the bike called "math," the bike called "higher-order thinking," the bike called "science"—but only if he or she refuses to give up.

Teachers can help students overcome their fear of failure by involving them in the development of mutually acceptable criteria and methods for measuring their progress. Teachers must encourage students to strive for the "3 Ds"—*determination, diligence,* and *discipline.*

Finally, teachers can use activities that build on the nonacademic strengths of students and take time to nurture and extol these strengths in the classroom (Marks, 1981). Students must know that they have opportunities to experience legitimate success when they effectively use and channel their nonacademic strengths. Once they realize they can strive for specific careers and professional goals that are based on their strengths, children are more likely to be motivated to overcome their academic deficiencies. Table 5.2 (page 112) presents some of the nonacademic strengths many Black and Hispanic students are likely to have, and indicates the possible academic or

Table 5.1

Lincoln's Setbacks and Successes

YEAR	SETBACKS	SUCCESSES
1832	• Lost job • Defeated for State Legislature	• Elected company captain of Illinois militia in Black Hawk War
1833	• Failed in business	• Appointed as postmaster of New Salem, IL • Appointed as deputy survey of Sangamon County
1834		• Elected to Illinois State Legislature
1835	• Sweetheart died	
1836	• Had nervous breakdown	• Re-elected to Illinois State Legislature • Received license to practice law in Illinois State Courts
1837	• Led Whig delegation in moving Illinois' state capital from Vandalia to Springfield • Became law partner of John T. Stuart	
1838	• Defeated for Speaker	• Nominated for Illinois House Speaker by Whig caucus • Re-elected to Illinois House • Served as Whig Floor Leader
1839		• Chosen presidential elector by first Whig convention • Admitted to practice law in U.S. Circuit Court
1840		• Argued first case before Illinois Supreme Court • Re-elected to Illinois State Legislature
1841		• Established own law practice with Stephen T. Logan
1842		• Admitted to practice law in U.S. District Court

Table 5.1 (continued)

Lincoln's Setbacks and Successes

YEAR	SETBACKS	SUCCESSES
1843	• Defeated in nomination for Congress	
1844		• Established own law practice with William H. Herndon as junior partner
1846		• Elected to Congress
1849	• Rejected for land officer	• Admitted to practice law in U.S. Supreme Court • Declined appointment as secretary and then as governor of Oregon Territory
1854	• Defeated for U.S. Senate	• Elected to Illinois State Legislature (but declined seat to run for U.S. Senate)
1856	• Defeated in nomination for Vice President	
1858	• Again defeated for U.S. Senate	
1860		• Elected President

career outlets that can be encouraged as a result of those strengths.

Help Students Overcome Their Rejection of Success

One of the most disturbing phenomena of the post-deseg-regation era has been the "rejection of success" on the part of many Black youth who seem to be unaware of the tremendous success numerous Black intellectuals and leaders have had through the years—even before Emancipation. All students, regardless of race or ethnicity, can benefit from history lessons

Table 5.2

Matching Nonacademic Strengths
With Career Choices

Nonacademic Strengths or Qualities	Possible Career Choices
• Moral responsibility	• Social services, teaching
• Compassion	• Psychology, medicine, nursing
• Diplomacy	• Politics
• Humor and wit	• Writing
• Verbal ability	• Law
• Sensitivity	• Counseling, teaching
• Independence	• Business, science
• Courage	• Civic activism, advocacy organization
• Altruism	• Social work, nursing, community organizing, environmental work
• Manual dexterity	• Computer science, carpentry, graphic arts
• Talent for innovation and improvisation	• Law, media, engineering, architecture, politics
• Mechanical talent	• Mechanics, plumbing, electrical work, drafting
• Expressive talent	• Performing arts, writing, interior design
• Culinary talent	• Chef, caterer, dietitian
• Physical prowess	• Firefighter, emergency medical technician, police officer
• Social talent	• Hotel management, sales

that show how Blacks struggled to succeed against the odds during the Jim Crow era from the 1870s through the 1950s. Historical accounts of the tremendous accomplishments of the "talented tenth" (a term used by Booker T. Washington to describe a group of Black individuals who were attending Black colleges in the late 1800s and early 1900s) can inspire many Black students to embrace, rather than reject, success. In my publication, *Dreaming of a P.H.A.T. Century*, I share many of those inspirational stories in an endeavor to inspire all youth to follow the exemplary success of many Blacks to overcome unbelievable obstacles to receive an education. Some Black slaves were beaten or lynched for learning how to read or for teaching others. Hispanic youth also must be reminded of the efforts of other Hispanics (locally or nationally) who strive for excellence and academic achievement in the face of seemingly insurmountable odds.

The sad reality, however, is that many Black and Hispanic youth encounter racism in contemporary desegregated settings and absorb the negative images they feel White society has of them. In short, they start believing the worst they hear about themselves. Many Black and Hispanic youth cope with these images and their feelings of discrimination, rejection, and exclusion from White society by developing an oppositional social identity. This "us versus them" mentality has a powerful impact on the aspirations of both Black and Hispanic youth.

In a study of low-income Black students in Washington, DC, high schools, Signithia Fordham and John Ogbu (1986) found that many Black students rejected success as a "White" behavioral norm or as a norm pleasing to teachers who most of these youth perceived as the enemy—even when the teacher was Black. Fordham and Ogbu found that the oppositional identity these students developed protected them from the perceived racism of the dominant culture. Consequently, these Black students ascribed certain behavioral norms as "White." The fear of being accused by their peers of abandoning their Black identity was cited as a major reason for many Black students refusing to study, shunning Standard English, and avoiding what they perceived as White interests (such as, the symphony, opera, and the humanities) (Fordham & Ogbu, 1986).

Fordham and Ogbu found that some Black students who did not want to typify White behavior were ambivalent toward academic success because they saw it as a "White prerogative." Many educational institutions have actually contributed to the belief held by some Black and Hispanic students that academic success is for Whites only through tracking, ability grouping, and programs that appear to students as discriminatory. Many Black and Hispanic students are made to feel they must "act White" to be successful (Fordham & Ogbu, 1986).

Adults can help Black and Hispanic students overcome this rejection of success that plagues them. This can be done through:

- Exposing students to successful Blacks and Hispanics

- Helping students become more goal-oriented

- Eliminating institutional racism

- Helping youth develop habits for success

Exposing students to successful Blacks and Hispanics. Teachers must help students understand and appreciate the fact that success is *definitely* part of the Black and Hispanic experience. Rather than foster the belief that academic achievement is a White prerogative, teachers must help Black and Hispanic students understand and appreciate the standards for excellence set by diverse races and cultures around the world. Black History and Hispanic History must be discussed year round so that *all* students can develop an understanding that success has *always* been a part of the racial and cultural history of these youth.

Helping students become more goal-oriented. Adults must help Black and Hispanic students understand *how* to be successful even when these students share their belief that they will not be welcome in mainstream America. Many Black and Hispanic youth who reject success simply do not know they can succeed in the White world, so they have not established short- or long-range goals. Many Black and Hispanic youth fail to set goals because they feel they have minimal control over their fate and will be unable to make a difference in the outcome of a problem, project, experiment, or grade (Beane, 1988). This belief, which is common to lower-income students, has been called an *external locus of control.* Many lower-income youth, as a result of school biases, see no relationship between hard work and success. Additionally, some Black and Hispanic students may have been taught by their parents that rewards very often can be discriminately and inconsistently dispensed (Howard, 1987). Some Black and Hispanic youth may even fail to set goals because they have little knowledge of what constitutes an acceptable goal.

Black and Hispanic students, especially, need to believe that goals are attainable and that their efforts will be rewarded. Educators can instill confidence in students by allowing them to set short-range goals for which they do receive support, recognition, and quick reward. More will be said about goal setting in the next section.

Eliminating institutional racism. If teachers are going to refute the notion among Black and Hispanic students that they cannot be successful or that they must choose between their own culture and that of the school, teachers also must take steps to eliminate institutional racism. Black and Hispanic youth are more likely to see academic achievement as a White prerogative when there is an overrepresentation of Blacks and Hispanics in special education classes or lower ability groups. Teachers and administrators must not only eliminate policies and programs that foster such overrepresentation, they should also:

- Review school policy and revise or eliminate rules that punish students for cultural habits, such as wearing African or cornrow hairstyles, signifying or playing the dozens, or being loud or expressive.

- Review instructional materials that belittle, exclude, or stereotype races and cultures. Add materials that are multicultural in all subject areas at all grade levels. If certain biased materials are kept, teachers must know how to use these materials in unbiased ways.

- Develop a basic familiarity with Black and Hispanic culture through staff-development sessions or personal efforts to enhance knowledge. Such efforts might include reading, visits to art shows or museums, and participating in social events for Black and Hispanic groups.

- Eliminate the word "minorities" from the vocabulary. Schools are preparing students for a world in which people of color are not in the minority at all.

- Use flexible, heterogeneous, and cooperative grouping rather than ability groupings and tracking.

- Do all you can do to ensure that schools in predominantly Black and Hispanic neighborhoods are financed at least at the same level as schools in predominantly White neighborhoods.

- Incorporate the provision of equal opportunity in the classroom as part of the teacher evaluation process.

- Most importantly, help Black and Hispanic students understand that school success will not require rejection of their home or family's culture.

Helping youth develop habits for success. Teachers can help youth focus on the future and overcome setbacks and adversity. In their book, *Think and Grow Rich: A Black Choice*, Dennis Kimbro and Napoleon Hill (1992) observe that while racial oppression and discrimination still exist, they should not keep Blacks or Hispanics from losing sight of the "greater battle" and developing themselves as individuals. In teaching Black and Hispanic youth to live inside and outside of their culture, people who are *Merchants of Hope* can help these students understand that "greatness is not measured by what a man or woman accomplishes, but by the opposition he or she has overcome to reach his or her goal" (Kimbro & Hill, 1992).

The academic self-image of some Black and Hispanic youth may be so low that they do not have the self-love needed to overcome real and perceived obstacles. A good and loving *Merchant of Hope* can open the door to student self-love and motivation. He or she can also help a student strengthen his personal resolve to use the talents he has to be a success. Effective and affirming *Merchants of Hope* can also help students gain knowledge and appreciation of others who have overcome seemingly insurmountable odds in their quest for greatness.

Teachers can also share with students the success principles outlined by Kimbro and Hill (1990). These principles include:

- Using the imagination wisely and putting ideas into action

- Having a burning desire to succeed and the right attitude

- Having faith—the prerequisite to power

- Developing persistence skills

- Developing a strong sense of self-worth

- Developing self-reliance and a better use of individual fortitude

- Developing a pleasing personality

- Getting and maintaining enthusiasm

- Setting goals and staying on track

- Developing and expanding the potential of the mind

Adults who interact with Black and Hispanic youth must help students appreciate these principles. Teachers can develop classroom activities and assignments around the application of these principles to everyday life. Parents, mentors, and *Merchants of Hope* can discuss these principles with youth as they engage them in completion of the Success Chart (See Table 5.3, page 120).

Set Short- and Long-Term Goals

Black and Hispanic students must be convinced that they can be what they choose to be in life. Teachers must help them understand that if they can conceive it in their hearts and believe it, they can achieve it. As noted previously, these students also must be taught the importance of persistence.

Table 5.3 is a Success Chart that can be used to help students set short- or long-term goals. This chart should be completed in the presence of the teacher. Students should first identify a goal they want to achieve by the age of 25. Next, students, with the help of the teacher, should list their outstanding qualities and those things that are likely to help them reach their goals. The teacher who has already identified at least three strengths the student possesses can share those strengths with the student at this time. The teacher can also discuss with students specific strategies for achieving their long-term goals. Teachers must also let students know that they want to help students reach their goals. As students identify weaknesses or those things that could hinder efforts to reach their goals, teachers can indicate a willingness to help overcome whatever weaknesses the students feel might be impeding their progress.

In addition to the use of this Success Chart, teachers can:

- Schedule a monthly show-and-tell session in which students share non-school-related goals they have set and accomplished.

- Have weekly reviews of famous Black and Hispanic Americans who have achieved their goals. Continue to remind students that success is very much a part of their culture and experience.

- Applaud all efforts students make to reach their goals.

- Set monthly academic achievement goals with and for each student and share them with parents or guardians.

Table 5.3

Success Chart

Student's Name_____

Goal:

List something you would like to have, become, or accomplish by the age of 25.

_____

_____

_____

_____

_____

_____

Help:

List qualities or characteristics you possess that will help you reach your goal.

_____

_____

_____

_____

_____

Hinder:

List things that could possibly limit your efforts to reach your goal.

_____

_____

_____

_____

_____

Strategies for achieving this goal:

1. _____
2. _____
3. _____
4. _____

This table can also be used to create short-range goals (for example, something you want to do within the next 3 weeks). For short-range goals, list the specific steps you need to take and include a time frame.

- Assist students in developing sequential strategies for meeting goals.

- Help students to see failure as a learning experience by discussing failure as part of the road to success.

Students can also be inspired by the role models they see in their teachers, especially their Black and Hispanic teachers. Far too many teachers are discouraged because they believe their students lack adequate role models in their homes and communities. Rather than concern themselves with the influences outside of the school which they cannot control, teachers can make the most of the time they have with students. Remember, most students spend more time interacting with their school family (approximately 6 hours every day) than they spend interacting with their families at home. A teacher's exemplary behavior and aspirations can have a tremendous influence on his or her students' drive and goal orientation.

Finally, teachers and administrators must be willing to reward students who fulfill their goals. Students are motivated by rewards; when success is rewarded, it is reinforced. For example, Eastern High School in Washington, DC, under former Principal Ralph Neal, annually sponsored four Student of the Month awards. The winners were top students who were recommended by teachers. Each winner received $15, a certificate, their pictures on a plaque in the school lobby, breakfast with a Kiwanis Club member, and lunch on Capitol Hill with the principal and a school board member. This program was designed to boost the self-image of students who were doing well and to make success a cultural norm for the school.

Educators must work very hard to dispel the belief that it does not pay to do well academically. Children can be motivated to succeed through inspirational examples. As often as possible, teachers should allow students to discuss local success stories, such as:

- The experiences of city or county council representatives who might have lived in the students' neighborhood or attended their school and who reached goals they set

- The accomplishments of elementary or high school alumni who also reached goals they set

- The triumphs of local businesspeople, community leaders, or family members who overcame setbacks

- The road to success taken by educators, including their own teachers

- The lives of national heroes, past and present, especially those whose early lives were similar to the student (See my book *Dreaming of a P.H.A.T. Century* for discussion of these success stories.)

Keep students inspired and let them know success can and will be theirs. They have to believe in their own abilities and the power within themselves in order to reach personal goals.

Develop Appropriate Teaching Styles

Many Black and Hispanic students respond favorably to extensive interaction with the teacher and other peers. I strongly encourage pats on the back and other gestures that may involve appropriate touching in a supportive and nurturing manner, especially for younger children. Teachers and school officials who are uncomfortable hugging students should learn how to "hug" students with their eyes. Loving looks and sincere smiles warm up the teaching environment, making it easier to enhance student motivation. Contact from the teacher to the student must be sincere and supportive— not intrusive. Teachers should also supplement the use of objects (such as, computers and other learning devices) with person-to-person interaction, proximity, and lots of assurance. In addition, teachers should be sure to:

- Speak in a comforting, consoling, but firm and determined voice

- Demonstrate fairness in the treatment of students

- Incorporate humor in their interaction with the class or individual students

- Develop rapport with students, and suggest that others do so as well

Maintain a high level of openness and acceptance with Black youth who engage in *stage setting*. These are activities deemed important and necessary by some Black youth before engaging in an assignment (such as, pencil sharpening, rearranging posture, checking paper and writing space, asking for repeat directions, and even checking perceptions with their neighbors). Many teachers are likely to perceive stage setting as an attempt to avoid work or disrupt class. However, this is an important activity for many Black youth (Gilbert & Gay, 1985). Teachers can convey their understanding and an acceptance of this need by allowing a few minutes for stage-setting maneuvers. This behavior stems from a field-dependent style of learning that calls for appropriate mood and setting before the youth can begin the performance.

Most importantly, teachers must show students that they have high expectations for their academic achievement. Telling them is not enough. Teachers can convince students that they believe in them and want them to excel by:

- Using the classroom walls to display the work of all students in areas where they are skilled

- Writing encouraging notes on students' papers and to parents or guardians

- Maintaining a warm, inviting classroom climate through the use of appropriate attitudes and behaviors and bright and bold colors at all grade levels

- Encouraging students' natural exuberance, and toning it down if necessary, without making students feel that they are wrong to show emotion

- Recognizing the knowledge and achievement of Black and Hispanic students in all areas

Scheduling one-on-one sessions with students to discuss their weekly, monthly, and long-range goals is also helpful. Teachers can monitor progress and provide insight for ongoing improvement. If a heavy class load precludes meeting with each student, meet with a significant number of students who require more attention.

According to Burnette (1999), the instructional strategies used with Black, Hispanic, and/or poor youth should also provide students with opportunities to learn in ways that are responsive to their own communication styles, cognitive styles, aptitudes, appearance, race, sex, disability, ethnicity, religion, socioeconomic status, and ability. The benefits of peer tutoring or peer coaching cannot be emphasized enough. Peer tutors can summarize the main points of each lesson and conduct necessary reviews to make certain comprehension has occurred before teachers present the next lesson.

The phrase "each one, teach one" should be a part of the class motto and should be embraced and internalized by every student. This is especially true for Black and Hispanic youth who come from cultures that place a high value on cooperation and relationships. Jaap (1999) found that mainstream values of independence and competition could actually impede learning in these youth.

Teachers should also make good use of the "Buddy Game," which calls for pairing students who will be "buddy" to one another. Students spend time with their buddies—getting homework assignments in their absence and learning and sharing skills, information, and strategies. Encourage buddies to each make a list of all the strengths and talents that make their buddies special.

Have a "King" or "Queen" for a day where every child gets to play the part of "Class King" or "Class Queen." (Choose by lottery or alphabetically.) The King or Queen's buddy comes before the class and takes a few minutes to share everything good they have learned about his or her buddy. The teacher also shares good things about who is being honored that day as King or Queen.

Use Homework and Television to Your Advantage

Homework should promote cooperation and communication among the teacher, student, and parent. It should help the child develop responsibility and independence, master a skill, and understand what has been taught. It should also encourage children to learn new things and keep parents informed about what their children are learning in school (Kuykendall, 1987).

Given the anticipated benefits of homework and television, teachers can make these activities more powerful experiences by:

- Giving students homework projects that can involve members of their families (for example, creating a family tree, assessing family strengths and virtues, and writing fictional stories that feature family members as heroes or heroines)

- Giving students homework assignments that incorporate their strengths. A student athlete who has difficulty reading might be asked to make an oral presentation in which he or she speculates which team might win the NBA Championship, Super Bowl, or World Series after reviewing and analyzing newspaper stories on professional sports teams and developing his or her own logical conclusions

- Allowing students to watch television programs they normally watch, even though such programs may be considered negative. Students can write a paper on what makes such programs inappropriate and what negative values those programs convey

- Giving students assignments that require viewing more documentaries, educational programs, and programs that address current issues

- Giving students homework assignments that will help them learn more about diverse cultures and races

- Giving students homework assignments that enhance character development and an understanding of such attributes as honesty, integrity, compassion, tenacity, tolerance, persistence, and resilience

Communicate to Ensure Your Real Intentions Are Understood

Cross-cultural miscommunication in the classroom does exist. Such miscommunication can lead to lower motivation and lower achievement, excessive speech/language therapy placements, perceptions of frequent, if unintentional, social insults from teachers and other students, frequent misunderstandings and misinterpretations from school personnel and other students, perception of negative school climate, and poor performance on tests and assessments (Taylor, 1987).

Teachers can avoid the consequences of cultural miscommunication by:

- Becoming a more effective listener—Keep an open, curious mind, and remember that, just like your students, you have two ears and one mouth for a reason.

- Focusing on the speaker's ideas while listening with feeling and intuition

- Becoming personally involved in what students say

- Asking for clarification when something is unclear

Remember, communication is conveyed from *total* person to *total* person. When we communicate, only 7% of what is conveyed comes from our words. Thirty-eight percent is nonverbal, conveyed through rate of speaking, tone, and volume. Fifty-five percent is non-vocal, through eye contact, body language, and posture (Weinberg & Catero, 1971). Do not make the mistake of using negative body language (arms folded across the chest, inattentive eyes, clenched jaw, and scowls) when you're trying to send a positive message. The child who tells a parent that "the teacher doesn't like me" has never heard the words. It is the teacher's *behavior*—non-vocal cues given to students—that causes them to feel disliked, disrespected, and demeaned. Teachers also communicate their expectations of students through a display (or lack thereof) of interest in the student's life, use of wait time (the time between the asking of a question and a student's response time; seven seconds is the norm), and their willingness to provide assistance upon request (Denbo, 1987).

Teachers also communicate expectations through facial expressions and eye contact. While some Black and Hispanic students may avoid direct eye contact with teachers out of respect, teachers must still help these youth develop the skill of using eye contact, for they will need it in the world of work. You can help students develop strong eye contact skills by giving them warm, encouraging eye contact. You can also use the following activity to strengthen students' use of eye contact.

Allow students to work in small groups where they will cut out photographs of eyes that they find in magazines or newspapers. Ask them to label what each set of eyes means—friendly eyes, fearless eyes, and so on. Post some of these eyes and their labels on a bulletin board. Students will be able to "look into eyes" throughout the day. This will become a habit-forming practice of looking into eyes. Believe me, it works!

Teachers must also give frequent, supportive feedback to students. Black and Hispanic students respond favorably to praise, assurance, encouragement, and supportive feedback. Teachers give positive feedback by:

- Acknowledging correct answers

- Discussing positive aspects of student performance

- Providing clues, repetition, or rephrasing for challenging or difficult questions

- Making students aware of specific areas of their performance where correction or improvement is needed

- Making suggestions for requisite improvement

Establish a Good School and Classroom Climate

The climates of the school and classroom are both critical in keeping students excited and motivated. Tardiness and truancy usually result when students find schools and classrooms to be demoralizing and debilitating because the adults in the school are cool and aloof. Children are "fair weather" just like adults. They will not rush to school to be greeted by "Hurricane Annie."

Chapter 7 provides more insight on the climate variables that affect behavior between students and teachers. The climates of both the school and the classroom should not only welcome students but should also keep them encouraged.

Strengthen Relations Between the Home and School

Although involvement of parents in the education of their children is essential to long-term school success, many teachers do little to encourage parental involvement and support—particularly when students are Black, Hispanic, or poor. The National Education Longitudinal Study of 1988 found that middle-income parents were four times more likely than low-income parents to be PTA members and twice as likely to have contacted their children's schools about academic matters (Scheider, Shiller, & Coleman, 1988).

As more school districts follow the leads of Cambridge, Massachusetts; Wake County, North Carolina; Manchester, Connecticut; La Crosse, Wisconsin; and San Francisco in desegregating schools based on socioeconomic criteria as opposed to race, teachers will need to do much more to encourage effective parental involvement among poorer parents who are still intimidated by educators (Fletcher, 2002). Teachers must also remember that many poor parents respond to the academic needs of their children the way their own parents responded to their academic needs. Many parents simply do not know what their roles should be. Every parent does not have parenting expertise. Many do not know what they should be doing in the home to enhance their child's achievement, motivation, or academic self-image. Parents have sometimes been socialized to believe that education is strictly the teacher's domain and that very little is required of them as parents. Teachers must reach out to parents and guardians, especially those who are Black, Hispanic, and poor, and make them feel comfortable about the role they will play as equal partners in the education of their children. More specific strategies on strengthening this delicate bond will be shared in chapter 8.

The Importance of Persistence

Many students who appear unmotivated will respond if the environment and the instructor are more conducive to learning. The tips presented herein will work only if teachers believe they can make a difference. Even when these steps are followed enthusiastically, some teachers still may not meet with immediate success. Educators must remember to use the same persistence we encourage in students. Once these tips are put into practice, student discipline may be less problematic. The chapters that follow provide additional insight on creating the most conducive environment for good student behavior and student and teacher success.

Chapter 6

The Need for Discipline

As a twig is bent the tree inclines.

—Virgil (Roman epic poet)

The need for effective classroom management includes the need to help students overcome obstacles to self-control and promote good self-discipline. While good behavior is necessary for all students to experience achievement, teachers have a better chance of increasing their students' motivation to achieve when they can develop in students a sense of responsibility, self-control, and the desire to achieve lifelong success.

The two basic causes of poor student behavior are internal (within the schools) and external (through family, peers, cultural influences, and other factors outside of the school).

Internal Causes of Poor Student Discipline

There are many school-related causes of student anger, rage, and concomitant bad behavior. Students are most likely to be disruptive and undisciplined as a result of school-related actions when they feel:

- Unwelcome

- Inferior

- Hopeless

- Victimized by the unjust, unfair behavior of school officials

- That bad behavior is expected

- The need to succeed at something

Feeling Unwelcome

If a student feels unwelcome or like an intruder, that student may demonstrate the need to be an integral part of the class through disruptive behavior. This desire for inclusion calls attention to the dominant need of the student for recognition. Students who feel unwelcome respond to the pain by modeling the behavior they feel teachers expect. Anger and meanness often develop when students feel they are unwelcome for no reason. Every effort must be made to make Black and Hispanic students feel appreciated, wanted, and welcome. Students are most likely to feel unwelcome when:

- The bulletin boards in school hallways and classrooms do not reflect students' history or culture.

- The climate of the school or classroom is not warm or inviting. (See chapter 7 for more information on creating a positive school and classroom environment.)

- Teachers or other adult school personnel act aloof, condescending, or negative toward the student for no apparent reason.

- There is a preponderance of students from their race in low-ability groups or tracks.

- They are ignored, isolated, or treated indifferently.

In the book, *Voices From the Classroom* (Olsen & More, 1982), many students who dropped out of school indicated they never felt welcome. Many cited negative teacher behavior as a reason for their desire to leave school early. Thus, in addition to causing disruptive behavior in some students, feeling unwelcome can also push students out of school.

Feeling Inferior

Quite often, disruptive students are responding to what they *perceive* as the teacher's belief in the student's inferiority. In such cases, students are likely to react with negative behavior that actually puts them in control of what happens in class. Similarly, some students satisfy their need for recognition, acceptance, appreciation, and inclusion by engaging in behavior that appears to be courting the rejection of the classroom teacher. Teachers should understand that many of these hostile and disruptive youth actually fear emotional slights from teachers. They may put up a hypersensitive defensive front to protect their feelings and emotions.

Feeling Hopeless

While it is true that some disruptive Black and Hispanic students are simply bored or restless, many are responding to or venting the rage they feel as a result of their loss of hope and their likely school failure. A truly hopeless child is likely to be a problem child as well. To augment the hope Black and Hispanic students need, teachers and schools must avoid institutional policies and programs, such as tracking or ability grouping, because they send signals of inferiority. Students are commonly placed in special education classes when it is the students' *behavior* rather than their ability that causes problems. This practice must be avoided if we are to help these students. When *Merchants of Hope* let students know they're willing to do whatever it takes to help individual students reach their full potential and goals they have set for life-long success, they remove from those students the anger, misplaced aggression, and disdain many of these Black and Hispanic youth often feel when they believe they have no future.

Feeling Victimized by Unjust, Unfair Treatment

As Black and Hispanic youth confront their racial and cultural identities and become more aware of the injustices that are often perpetuated because of race, they often develop resentment and anger. The oppositional identity many Black and Hispanic youth display often results because they have witnessed or experienced unfair treatment. It is not unusual for children of color to respond negatively to what they may perceive as unequal or unfair treatment. Selective rule enforcement, where some students are disciplined and other students are excused for committing the same infraction, must be eradicated altogether.

Certainly, there may be times when school personnel will feel there has been no unjust or unfair treatment even though a student or parent may feel otherwise. In those cases, school personnel must keep in mind that perceptions can't be disputed. However, they can be changed. Sincere dialogue is necessary, and school officials must show evidence of fairness. For example, if a Black student asserts that he or she has been suspended for the same behaviors that did not result in suspension for a White student, school officials must offer proof that such unjust treatment did not occur. If there is no evidence to dispute a perception of unfairness, school officials should acknowledge that they are unable to dispute the claim but will use this information of perceived bias to develop staff training, policy, procedures, and practices to eradicate any bias—perceived or otherwise. You need to show that fairness within your organization is important and that you're prepared to make changes in policy and practice to prove it.

Feeling That Bad Behavior Is Expected

The self-fulfilling prophecy about behavior still holds true in our schools. It is important that teachers do not communicate preconceived notions about behavioral tendencies or suggest that Black and Hispanic students are bad, uncouth, or more likely to misbehave than White students. If they do, the students are likely to behave accordingly.

Feeling a Need to Succeed at Something

The failure to provide students with frequent opportunities for success and accomplishment in the classroom is another contributing factor to poor behavior. Black, Hispanic, and poor students have a need to show what they can do, just as other students take pride in showing their work. If students are not given frequent opportunities for success through classroom activities, they are likely to satisfy the need for accomplishment by telling jokes or disrupting class.

The need for achievement is paramount. If students are struggling academically, teachers should give them opportunities for success in utilizing whatever nonacademic strengths they have. For example, those with strengths such as leadership or human-relations skills can use these qualities in facilitating classroom activities or discussions. To prevent the class clown from successfully disrupting class, the teacher must provide an opportunity for some form of classroom success for that student. He or she may be called on to come before the class and lift spirits with a little humor, develop humorous phrases or positive messages that reflect class spirit, or develop humorous insights into what the class is learning in a way that reinforces the instruction. When under-achieving students are successfully engaged in constructive classroom endeavors, they are less likely to be successful at venting their learning frustrations through disruptive and annoying actions in the classroom.

School personnel can minimize student anger and pro-clivity for disruptive behavior by:

- Treating students with dignity and respect

- Teaching students to behave responsibly

- Understanding and responding appropriately to habitual behavior

- Giving students more of what they need

- Modeling the behavior you expect

Treating students with dignity and respect. Remember, even when youth do bad things, they do not want to be belittled in front of others. Frequent ridicule or name-calling will lead to hostility, anger, resentment, and disruptive behavior. In his book *What Do I Do When . . . ?*, Allen Mendler admonishes educators to maintain strong bonds with students so as not to destroy student dignity when taking requisite disciplinary actions (1992).

Teaching students to behave responsibly. Some Black, Hispanic, and poor youth may have been socialized to believe that some of their behavioral norms are acceptable. Quite often, when students appear to misbehave in school, they are actually displaying behavior that is acceptable in their subculture. Some students simply have not been taught appropriate school behavior. The popular book *All I Really Need to Know I Learned in Kindergarten* (Fulghum, 1993) discusses behavior not only appropriate for school, but for lifelong success, such as sharing and not talking out of turn. Many youth who show irresponsible behavior or a lack of self-control in school can still be taught how to conduct themselves in a classroom setting. They may not have learned appropriate behavior in kindergarten or primary grades, but they must still be socialized in schools.

Understanding and responding appropriately to habitual behavior. Some behavior results from habit. I have seen students punished for sucking or gritting their teeth, twitching, or making clicking sounds. These behaviors are habitual nervous reactions students may be unable to control. An understanding adult can calm the student's nerves by ignoring such reactions. Similarly, if a student is chronically tardy to school or class, teachers can discuss this behavior privately with the student rather than embarrass or demean the student in front of the class.

Giving students more of what they need. When students feel that teachers really care about them and appreciate their presence, they are less likely to misbehave. Remember, all students, regardless of race or class, need affection, appreciation, approval, achievement, and accomplishment. Teachers, counselors, administrators, and other adults must show appreciation of improved student behavior, effort, and attitude. Importantly, students must be reminded that their presence is wanted and their nonacademic strengths have been observed and are appreciated. Comments such as those that follow will certainly enhance students' feelings of affection, appreciation, and approval:

- "Maria, I am so very pleased to see you today. We missed you while you were out sick."

- "Your behavior today was very good, Pedro. Thank you for making my day."

- "What a kindhearted young man you are, Antar. I enjoy having you in my class."

- "Thank you, Zakaria, for showing such determination. You may not have completed the assignment, but I know how hard you tried."

Modeling the behavior you expect. Teachers often contribute to poor student behavior when they display anger, impatience, intolerance, arrogance, disdain, disrespect, and other behaviors for which students are often disciplined. Teachers must learn self-control if they are, in fact, to facilitate self-control in students.

External Causes of Poor Student Discipline

Factors outside of school contribute to what may appear to be antisocial or anti-White behavior in some Black or Hispanic youth. Some causes of poor student discipline are rooted in family and home influences, cultural influences, and peer pressure.

Family and Home Influences

While most teachers expect that parents will play a major role in disciplining their children, some parents are unable to instill the values or develop the character required in their children for appropriate school behavior. Some of these parents even have given up on their children. Does this mean the schools should give up, too? No, it does not.

Some families actually reward children—or give tacit approval—to behavior that the school might find unacceptable. For example, some youth may come from homes where parents encourage speaking out, telling jokes, questioning rules, fighting back, or laughing out loud. In such instances, we cannot blame children for their lack of awareness of the cultural and communication norms valued by our educational institutions. We must help them to understand and appreciate appropriate behavioral norms without giving the impression that we are demanding conformity or that we dislike them because of their behavior. In addition, parent awareness conferences between school officials and parents can be held to make certain that parents understand acceptable and unacceptable school behavior.

Cultural Influences

Many youth are very susceptible to antisocial messages heard in rock, rap, and other forms of music. Moreover, messages sent through the behavior of other adults, governments, or institutions have a subliminal effect on what students feel is acceptable behavior. Helping students understand the difference between self-defense and aggression is critical. For example, some students may feel that "pre-emptive attacks" on other students are warranted if they think the other student is trying to harm them. Teachers should engage students in discussions about what constitutes legitimate self-defense. Self-defense is warranted only after a student has been attacked, struck first, or is about to be attacked imminently. Students must be made to understand that they cannot allow suggestions from others to dictate their behavior. This is true no matter whether those suggestions come from rap artists, music, movies, television stars, or even their own parents or teachers—if their suggestions do not have the child's best interests at heart.

Peer Pressure

Peer groups obviously play a big role in mitigating or enhancing behavioral problems. As noted previously, many youth develop an "us versus them" mentality when they think the school has already rejected them. These students feel that the only support they have comes from peers who see teachers as the enemy. Schools must break down this alienation, or discipline problems will continue. Teachers can influence students and their rebellious peer groups through strategies designed to reflect genuine concern, support, and some understanding. Remember, oppositional identities are formed when students feel most alienated.

Strategies for Discipline Problems

Adults who seek to minimize or eradicate discipline problems in Black, Hispanic, and poor students must:

- Check their own attitudes first.

- Use preventive classroom strategies.

Checking Your Attitude

While it may be hard to believe, there are teachers who do not like every child in his or her class. This dislike is perceived not only by that student, but also by other students. Teachers who find it difficult to like a particular child should seek instead to love the humanity in that child. Remember, many Black and Hispanic students who develop an oppositional identity have been offended and even hurt by the insensitive comments or actions of school officials (Tatum, 1997).

Collins, Tamarkin, and Haley (1990) suggest telling poorly disciplined children on a daily basis what you like about them and then seek to discern what they like about themselves.

When students know there is a bond of genuine admiration and appreciation, they are more receptive to suggestions from teachers regarding behavior that might be changed. Once adequate bonding has occurred, teachers can get students to discuss behavior they would like to change or improve in themselves. Teachers also should develop the attitude that *there are no bad children, just inappropriate behaviors.*

Teachers will be unable to implement strategies and activities that will prevent student misbehavior if they believe:

- Most Black and Hispanic youth are just bad kids.

- A good student is a quiet student.

- A good class is a class where there is no active learning, movement, or student interaction.

- Students learn best when there is no class noise.

- Children are being disrespectful when they challenge a teacher's fairness.

- All youth who crack jokes, laugh loudly, or do not conform in dress, personal appearance, or dialect are underachievers.

Remember, youth respond to adults based on how they think adults will respond to them or have responded in the past.

Administrators and school personnel who harbor the above feelings about Black, Hispanic, or poor youth should think about their motivations for being educators. Administrators who recognize these qualities in members of their teaching staff should consider whether they want these staff members in their schools.

Using Preventive Strategies

Once students get the message that their education and lifelong success are the school's priority, they are more likely to respond with favorable and positive behavior. This message is conveyed through the effective use of teaching styles that have a positive impact on student motivation. Many schools and classrooms are not structured to facilitate the achievement of some Black and Hispanic students. Classrooms are still predominantly "teacher centered" as opposed to "student centered." Many teachers still engage in behavior that suggests they are uncomfortable with the existence of diverse populations in their schools. Even in some all-Black schools, some Black teachers have been known to behave towards some of their lower-class students in ways that suggest the student is not wanted. As indicated previously, student reaction to perceived indifference is predictably negative.

The following strategies can help teachers keep students from becoming discipline problems:

- Make certain you have taken time with the student to discuss one-on-one the student's lifelong goals and how the experience in your class will help the student reach those lifelong goals. Use the Success Chart presented in Table 5.3 (page 120) with students who tend to misbehave.

- Remember, all children have a special gift or talent. Creative and effective teachers are able to augment student motivation by providing opportunities for each of these gifted students to shine. By doing this, teachers are able to offset the negative actions of children who are seeking recognition in the classroom.

- School officials and parents must also make certain students understand that success is a process, not just a destination. Teachers should assign class projects for potentially disruptive youth that not only build on that child's individual and cultural strengths but will also satisfy their need for success. For example, students can be given the assignment of describing their own experiences and contrasting them with the experiences of other students. Students might also be given the assignment of responding to open-ended questions, such as "What do you think would have happened if . . . ?" Such an activity will not only provide an opportunity for successful completion, it will also enhance students' critical-thinking skills.

- Enhance responsibility by giving students a role to play in maintaining a manageable classroom. Many students are unmotivated and disruptive because of teacher behavior that stresses adult domination and student obedience (McClelland, 1990). According to research by McClelland, adult domination occurs when adults prescribe what a youth is to do and how it is to be done. McClelland also concluded that adults who stress obedience and conformity in order to develop "polite and manageable" children inadvertently lower their students' motivation to achieve (1990).

- Enhance the clarification of positive values and improve responsible behavior in Black and Hispanic students by making them a part of the rule-enforcement process. Teachers can divide students into small work groups and give each group the task of determining, as a group, 10 rules that should govern all classroom behavior. Each group also must agree on appropriate consequences for rule violations. Each small group then presents to the class the rules and consequences they developed. Students should be given newsprint paper and markers to record their decisions. Once every group has presented its consensus of appropriate rules and the reasons for them, all students vote on the rules and consequences that will govern their behavior. Then post a complete list of rules and consequences in a prominent place in the classroom for everyone to see.

This activity will improve student behavior by giving students a feeling of ownership for the structure and operation of the classroom. More importantly, it will enhance the students' sense of responsibility, their acceptance of positive values and behavioral norms, and the cohesion among students in the classroom. Children are more likely to support and encourage other children when they share responsibility, purpose, and common values.

- Show students you respect them—both individually and collectively. Establish trusting relationships with students. Collins, Tamarkin, and Haley (1990) suggest making friends with students, complimenting them, letting them know how much they were missed when they have been absent, and even sitting with them during lunch. Teachers also can take time to discuss with students any real or perceived problems that they may be having at home, in the school (with other teachers or students), or in other environments.

What to Do When Students Continue to Misbehave

Even when a teacher feels he or she has been supportive, respectful, and caring, students may still behave inappropriately. Teachers should understand that many Black and Hispanic youth often are socialized with attitudes and strategies designed to enhance their survival in a White environment that is more often than not perceived to be hostile. These students are taught to appreciate some skills and behavioral norms that are not always condoned in our classrooms. Some of those skills that may be prized in their respective communities, but not in our schools, include nonverbal communication, dance and rhythmic movements, rapping, learning through cooperative dependence on others, and verbal interplay during instruction.

Teachers must still socialize Black and Hispanic students to live both inside and outside of their own cultural groups. However, teachers risk further alienation when they refuse to understand or appreciate the cultural values, norms, and communication patterns these youth bring to the learning environment.

Even when students behave inappropriately, teachers may be able to use adverse behavior as an opportunity to facilitate student growth and acceptance of corrective behavioral norms. The following tips should help.

Punish the Behavior, Not the Person

It is important to distinguish between the behavior and the person. Teachers must inform students constantly—through spoken and written reminders and supportive behavior—that they respect and admire students as individuals. Once students understand that the consequences are for inappropriate behavior rather than the students' existence, they are more likely to modify the behavior and to accept the guidance of well-meaning adults. I recall that when I was a young and sometimes quite mischievous child, my mother would remind me of her intense love for me, even when she was acknowledging her strong dislike for inappropriate behavior. I continued to do this as a parent and teacher.

Discipline Students With a Firm but Loving Touch

If there is no love, no genuine concern, no desire to help, the disciplinary act is likely to lead to bitterness and resentment, not maturity (Collins, Tamarkin, & Haley, 1990). Renowned educators Collins, Tamarkin, and Haley (1990) offer the following strategies for dealing with disruptive students:

- Ask students to write compositions or deliver 3-minute speeches on some aspect of their inappropriate or disruptive behavior. For example, a student guilty of gum chewing might be asked to write a composition on the etymology of gum, rather than writing punitive lines such as, "I will not chew gum in class."

- Continue to reward and compliment students for good behavior and take extra teaching time, either before or after school, to help students who are slower and more likely to misbehave.

I was not the most disciplined student in my early grades. I remember being punished by many teachers because I was an incessant "talker." Most of my teachers would make me write 500 times, "I will not talk in class" and bring it back the next day signed by my mother. While I detested this form of punishment, it obviously did little to help. My proclivity for talking never ceased—until the fifth grade. I have already shared the story of how one teacher, Mrs. Ruth Odom (a very wise and loving fifth-grade teacher), was able to identify and build on what she saw as a strength. She told me that I had a "gift of gab." Jokingly, she once remarked, "If we could get you out of fifth grade, one day you'll make a lot of money talking!" Rather than punish me the way other teachers had, she asked me to do a 5-minute oral presentation on public speaking. I remember working very hard on the speech I was to give. More importantly, however, I remember that after giving my oral presentation, Mrs. Odom and my classmates cheered for me. Not only did Mrs. Odom enhance my academic self-image, she also developed a nonacademic strength I did not realize I had. Moreover and most importantly, she gave me the desire to behave appropriately and focus on my future.

I'm glad I listened to Mrs. Odom, and I'm extremely grateful that she turned a negative behavior into a positive opportunity for development. As a result of her firm but gentle guidance and her desire to help me learn from inappropriate behavior, I became a model student who went on to excel in a number of ways. When I became a teacher, I used similar activities when students misbehaved. I found students were more likely to modify bad behavior when they were allowed to learn or develop a skill, talent, or gift—as a result of the inappropriate behavior.

Use Creative Alternatives to Suspension, Detention, and Isolation

Many school districts use alternative suspension programs or in-school suspension. Quite often, however, even these well-meaning alternatives defeat their purpose. In many in-school suspension programs, students simply go to a room with other disruptive students and a caretaker adult where they are allowed to do everything except learn from their behavior.

In such alternative suspension programs, students should be asked to prepare papers on the impact of their behavior on other students, how their behavior has detracted from their pursuit of legitimate lifelong goals, or how a modification of behavior might make them better people. Most importantly, students should be disciplined in such a way that they cannot distance themselves completely from the learning process. Unless students are given opportunities to assess the impact of their behavior and to analyze reasons for behavioral change, such practices as in-school suspension will do more harm than good.

Making Positive Changes

Teachers will always have to deal with mischievous and disruptive students. Even when students display a mischievous streak, however, they still deserve opportunities for transformation and academic growth. A good teacher can make certain such opportunities are always a part of the school day.

Teachers, administrators, and school personnel can abate many of the internal causes of poor student discipline by working together to make the physical appearance of their respective school appealing and inviting. However, only positive behavior can alleviate the feeling of being unwelcome. With fairness, outreach, and sincerity, school officials can warm students' hearts, bond more effectively with them, and reduce bad behavior. When students' needs are met, they are less likely to misbehave. When school officials have an understanding of home, peer, and other outside influences, they are better able to implement appropriate intervention and prevention measures. Even when students continue to misbehave after all other efforts have failed, educators must not give up their efforts to transform these young lives. These efforts will take time, but improving the internal and external climate of the school, as well as the home-school bond, will help tremendously.

Chapter 7

Creating a Positive School and Classroom Climate

I have come to a frightening conclusion that I am the decisive element in the classroom. It is my personal approach that creates the climate, my daily mood that makes the weather . . .

—Haim Ginott (1969)

If you have ever experienced genuine "emotional warmth" or felt "emotionally cold"—regardless of what the thermostat says—you'll understand that climate is not always contingent on temperature. Most assuredly, how we feel emotionally in a particular physical setting is determined not only by room appearance (colors, lighting, arrangement of furniture) but also by the relationships and interactions of the individuals in that particular setting.

All of us, especially children, respond emotionally to our physical surroundings. While colors have been shown to evoke certain feelings and emotions in adults, it is also true that colors and other physical elements have a strong impact on moods and behavior in children. A good school climate can generate enthusiasm, clarify values, build confidence, and strengthen relationships. Through the school and class-room climate, students are often inspired, nurtured, sup-ported, and comforted. A negative school climate can foster hostility, alienation, underachievement, and hopelessness. Teachers and administrators must make certain that the classroom and school climates neither stifle student growth nor destroy student confidence. Since climate is determined not only by physical appearance, but also by human interac-tion and the prevailing conditions affecting activities, school officials must make sure schools and classrooms incorporate climate conditions and variables conducive to student and teacher success.

Physical Conditions

Children who attend school in dilapidated, antiquated, and poorly kept facilities are likely to feel the psychological effects of inequitable school resources. The push during the 1970s to outlaw intra-district disparities in school financing was largely a result of the concern parents, administrators, and policymakers had over the impact that these disparities, which were in some cases blatant, were having on student attitudes about attending school.

The first consideration for school officials who are serious about creating a motivational climate is to make certain that students can feel proud of the school's physical facility. Despite the appearance of the surrounding community, stu-dents should still have reason to feel pride in the physical condition of the school.

Unfortunately, many Black and Hispanic youth live in areas (both urban and rural) where there has not only been serious deterioration, but there has also been what I consider to be malignant neglect by city, state, and federal officials. In his book, *Savage Inequalities*, Jonathan Kozol documents this blight and neglect in some selected cities. For example, Kozol found that predominantly Black East St. Louis, Missouri, is home for some of the sickest children in America (1991, p. 20). He also reports that:

- Sewage back-ups frequently flood schools.

- Gaseous fumes are being emitted from the pipes under some schools, making people ill.

- Former governor Jim Thompson told the press he would not pour money into East St. Louis to solve their long-term problems.

- The chairman of the St. Louis Board remarked that "East St. Louis is simply the worst possible place . . . to have a child brought up."

In New York City, Kozol found blatant inequities in per pupil expenditures between New York's poorest districts, where per pupil expenses average $5,500, and its wealthiest districts, where per pupil expenses were as high as $11,000. Indeed, in some suburban districts within New York State, per pupil expenses were as high as $15,000. The disparity between allocations granted by state legislators to school districts shows similar neglect. Some poor school districts in New York City receive as little as 90 cents per pupil for legislative grants while wealthier districts receive as much as $14.00 per pupil (1991).

Whether the discussion focuses on schools in Camden or Compton, Dallas or Denver, the Mississippi Delta or the farmlands of the Midwest, disparities still exist between funds allocated for children in poor districts and those in wealthier districts. Kozol argues that because of the "extraordinary miseries of life" in some blighted urban districts, children who attend schools in these districts should receive more than children who attend schools in wealthy districts—not half as much, which is what many actually receive. Kozol also warns of the "psychological disarray of children growing up in burnt out housing, walking past acres of smoldering garbage on their way to school" and attending underfunded, neglected schools (1991, p. 37).

School officials who are serious about motivating Black and Hispanic students to succeed academically can still instill pride in these students—even when their schools reflect malignant neglect from local, state, county, and federal officials. Kozol found many heartwarming stories of wonderful teachers and students who are succeeding against the odds. In schools that are predominantly Black, Hispanic, or poor, students must be reminded incessantly of their promising potential. Students and parents must also be reminded of local efforts to get state, county, or federal officials to improve their schools.

While the local community waits for state, county, or federal assistance, or while teachers and parents wait for their school boards and administrators to repair old, dilapidated school buildings, educators can still encourage students, concerned parents, and community leaders to take part in efforts to make the school building and surrounding campus more aesthetically pleasing. Teachers can develop gardening and landscaping classes. They can also use student artwork to enhance the physical appearance of a building while waiting for general repairs. Allowing students to be a part of efforts to beautify a school building will give them more ownership of the school and enhance their desire to improve other aspects of that school as well.

When students are pleased with the physical structure, they are more comfortable about being in school. Students have been known to react negatively when ridiculed by other youth for attending old, dilapidated, run-down schools. School officials should not be surprised when students are truant or show little desire to attend schools that are dilapidated, overcrowded, cold, and generally uninviting. While the exterior of the school building is important, we all know it's what's on the inside that really counts.

The Internal Climate of the School

The correlates for effective schooling include an emphasis on establishing a good school learning climate (Hale-Benson, 1982). A good school climate features:

- A positive commitment of *all* staff to student achievement

- Recognition of diverse gifts and talents in students

- Establishment of appropriate standards of behavior

- Provision of a safe and orderly environment

A Positive Commitment of All School Staff to Student Achievement

It is important that individual teachers be committed to each one of their students. However, when this commitment exists in all adult school staff, a climate is established where every student knows he or she is expected to do well and will not be allowed to be less than his or her best.

A total school approach to educating Black and Hispanic students must involve all school personnel in the socialization of these youth. Cafeteria workers, custodians, engineers, secretaries, bus drivers, nurses, crossing guards, and other support staff must understand the impact of their behavior and biases on student performance and motivation. If students or parents feel they are unwelcome, unappreciated, or disrespected by school personnel, their desire to please and bond with adults in the school is likely to deteriorate as is their academic performance (see chapter 4).

Not only must all adults in the school communicate their respect, appreciation, and belief in every child, the school itself also must convey a positive message of hope. This can be done through the use of bulletin boards, murals, walls of fame, display boards for student work, school slogans, pep rallies that encourage excellence in all areas, school songs, and other school-spirit activities.

Recognition of Diverse Gifts and Talents in Students

More than anything else, students must believe they can succeed in their school setting. The school must implement programs that reflect its appreciation of the diverse gifts and talents in all students. In many gifted-and-talented programs, children are identified as gifted only if they show above average cognitive skills. However, many Black and Hispanic youth are especially gifted in nonacademic areas and should be allowed the opportunity to develop those gifts as well.

Schools can create clubs and programs for youth who show special gifts, including the following:

- Comedy Club (for class clowns)

- Current-Issues Debate Team (for excessive talkers)

- Rappers Forum (for poets and rappers)

- Leaders Forum (for students who may not show academic skills but who are recognized as leaders by their peers)

- "New You" Club (for male and female students whose strength seems to be personal adornment, style, and cosmetology)

- Designers Club (for students interested in designing clothes and fashions)

- Artists' Alley (for students who exhibit special skills in art)

- Music Makers Club (for students who play instruments)

- Future Engineers Club (for students with mechanical abilities)

This list is not exhaustive. Take time at your school to discuss the creation of clubs that can strengthen the talents and enhance the gifts of all students.

School programs and activities that allow students to shine in doing whatever they do best will not only keep students excited about being in school, but will also foster a climate of welcome and warmth.

Establishment of Appropriate Standards of Behavior

The previous chapter on discipline shares some of the school-related causes of poor discipline. School officials can greatly improve the climate for classroom management and student behavior when standards of behavior are developed with student and community input. Students who feel they have been unjustly treated in a school environment are likely to reduce their efforts to succeed in that environment. Students who display aloofness, hostility, indifference, and even meanness are often mirroring the coolness they feel from adults or other students in the school. When there are no standards for student behavior, students are more likely to feel adults are picking on them when they do not perform. In the case of Black and Hispanic youth, standards of behavior (and the enforcement of rules across the board) are more likely to send the message that no student will be singled out and there will be no uneven application of rules and enforcement strategies.

In establishing appropriate standards of behavior, school policymakers and officials should first convene a task force of parents; students; teachers; and civic, social, religious, and community leaders to determine what student behaviors are inappropriate. Many schools have discipline handbooks or codes that are so outdated they no longer reflect the needs of contemporary school children. By allowing the community to help develop a revised handbook or code, administrators can facilitate development of a "community of caring," where significant community representatives can have a collective influence not just on student behavior, but also on collective community action designed to enhance student motivation and achievement.

School leaders must share with parents the primary concern of the school. Is it motivation and achievement, or is it the maintenance of good student behavior and public relations? School officials should make sure every parent is instructed (perhaps during the first visit with the classroom teacher) on the contents of the discipline handbook or the school code of conduct. Moreover, every classroom teacher must take time to discuss school rules and consequences for violating the code during class instruction. The distinction should be made about the difference between enforcing school rules and developing and enforcing class rules. Importantly, school officials must make certain Black and Hispanic students are not disciplined unfairly and are not singled out for the poor behavior of an entire class or group.

Provision of a Safe and Orderly Environment

When there are standards of behavior that reflect student, parent, and community concerns, schools are better able to develop a welcoming climate. The establishment of a purposeful, safe, and orderly environment is important for providing the sense of security and protection students must have in order to feel good about being in a school building. However, school officials must rethink their definition of an orderly environment. Children should feel safe but should not be made to feel as though they are in prison. Howard (1987) emphasized that there should be more activity, movement, and sharing during some of the learning experiences of Black and Hispanic youth. This means that order might, by necessity, be defined as that which fosters student motivation. Through standards of behavior, schools can establish a code that determines hall behavior, bathroom behavior, lunchroom behavior, playground behavior, and so on. However, it is important that teachers and students be allowed to establish class rules and corresponding procedures for enforcing the rules (see chapter 6). Otherwise, students are less likely to feel ownership of the classroom and more likely to develop an "us versus them" mentality.

Classroom Climate

The learning environment should enhance rather than harm the academic self-image of students. Several factors must be considered when establishing an appropriate classroom learning environment. As with school climate, these factors can be characterized in terms of the *physical setting* and *teacher behavior.*

Physical Setting

Classrooms must not only be comfortable, they must also create an atmosphere in which all students can become excited about their achievement and future goals. Care must be taken by educators to have appropriate lighting, ventilation, and temperatures. It does not matter whether your school population is integrated or of only one race; the classroom climate should still reflect an appreciation of diversity. To reinforce learning and enhance excitement, the physical setting should include such things as:

- Colorful decorations with warm, bold colors

- Positive slogans that foster values, inspire students, and facilitate persistence

- Information on the accomplishments and contributions of Black, Hispanic, Native American, and Asian leaders; inventors; civil, social, and human rights leaders; and other heroes and heroines—This class wall should remain all year, not just in September for Spanish Heritage Month or February for Black History Month. In high schools, this wall can feature information and pictures of Blacks, Hispanics, and other people of color who have contributed in particular subject areas (such as science and English). Make sure that other walls in the school reflect contributions of Blacks, Hispanics, and other people of color in all walks of life and professional areas.

- Displays of individual work and accomplishments—During the year, every child should see something he or she has done posted on the wall.

- Learning stations with resource materials

The physical setting should also be conducive to student-student and student-teacher interaction. It helps if children are not seated one behind the other and if they have movable chairs. Teachers can facilitate student pride in their classroom by encouraging cleanliness and student ideas on how to beautify the learning environment.

A highly decorated classroom alone will not keep Black and Hispanic students motivated. The behavior of the teacher is most significant in determining how comfortable and excited these students will be in the learning environment.

Teacher Behavior

In previous chapters I emphasized the powerful impact of teacher behavior on student attitudes and behavior. In her assessment of teacher expectations on student achievement, Sheryl Denbo (1986) describes climate variables as "teacher behaviors which affect student attitudes toward self, and teacher behaviors that build or destroy respect between students and teachers" (p. 97). As Ginott (1969) noted, quite accurately, the teacher's daily mood makes the weather. Teachers can create a warm, encouraging classroom climate by fostering:

- Mutual trust and respect between students

- Mutual helpfulness between students

- Acceptance and appreciation of student differences and diversity

- Freedom of student expression

Mutual trust and respect between students. When teachers are disrespectful to some students, they create a climate where other students feel it is permissible to show disrespect also. In a study by Ray Rist (1972), high-achieving students in a classroom where students were grouped by ability belittled students labeled as low-achievers—following the model of interaction set by the classroom teacher. Other experts, including Brophy and Good (1974), have commented on the failure of many teachers to set an example that reflects courtesy and respect for all youth.

The "us versus them" mentality that exists in many schools reflects the animosity between Black and Hispanic youth and school officials, and often carries over to student-student relationships. If made to feel inferior by other students who may or may not be modeling adult behavior, some Black and Hispanic students may respond with verbal attacks. Similarly, a lack of trust between teachers and students is likely to create a lack of trust between students. The end result—the worst-case scenario—is an integrated school where segregation, classism, and elitism still exist. In attempting to explain the self-segregation of Black youth, Tatum (1997) found that this racial grouping in a racially mixed setting is a developmental process in response to an environment stressor—racism.

Joining with one's peers for support in the face of such stress is a positive coping strategy. School officials must foster trust between students of different races and classes through their own exemplary behavior if they want to minimize the environmental stress and the need for coping strategies experienced by many students of color. When students are unable to trust or respect each other, they are unlikely to support one another or develop the mutually interdependent relationships that can foster achievement gains and coexistence in a diverse society. I should emphasize here that a school climate that fosters mutual trust and respect between students is necessary to reduce the alienation many non-conforming White students are likely to feel as well. School shootings in Colorado, Arkansas, and Oregon in the late 1990s were committed by alienated White youth who felt a need to hurt students and adults.

Mutual helpfulness between students. I have previously discussed the merits of heterogeneous grouping, cooperative learning, peer tutoring, and peer coaching. When teachers provide opportunities for students to work together, they foster an improved climate, making it more likely that student performance will be enhanced. A climate that establishes mutual support, helpfulness, and interdependence between students is created more easily when teachers:

- *Use praise and affirmation in communicating with all students.* Research has shown that Black and Hispanic students receive less teacher praise and more teacher criticism than White students (Dunkin & Biddle, 1974). Even when Blacks and Hispanics give a right answer, those who are perceived as under-achievers are still less likely to be praised than students perceived as high achievers (Good & Brophy, 1973). A study by David and Myra Sadker (1985) found that teachers were more likely to say, "Okay," to Black students than to White students, whether or not their answer was correct, thus leaving the Black student with little information about the quality of his or her performance. Teachers who continue to display such obvious signs of bias are only encouraging negative interaction among students. Hare (2001) found that the negative differential treatment of Black students by

White teachers is still the major cause of alienation and poor school discipline among many Black youth.

- *Are physically close to their students.* Physical proximity also is important. While there are different cultural perceptions of the need for physical touching and closeness in the classroom, there is an abundance of research indicating that physical closeness, for the most part, is a good teaching technique. Students who are physically closest to the teacher receive more academic and nonacademic attention (Denbo, 1986).

Teachers cannot be expected to change their seating charts daily. However, a good teacher will move around the class so that every child feels some proximity. In doing this, teachers send a message to all students that every child is an integral and welcome part of the learning environment. All too often, when teachers are in close proximity to underachieving students, it is to dominate them, discipline them, or degrade them. When physical closeness conveys a spirit of support and helpfulness, other students are more likely to feel a desire to offer similar help and support.

- *Use student recommendations to facilitate cooperation.* Student recommendations should be used to monitor student progress. Given what we know about test bias, it is important that educators look at alternative means of monitoring student progress. Students can (and should) be encouraged to participate in non-testing techniques that allow them to provide teachers with information about what they and other students are learning (Lezotte & Bancroft, 1985). Through the use of the Buddy Game (see chapter 5), heterogeneous grouping/cooperative learning, think-pair-share (where students discuss their analyses with a partner before opening their thoughts up for class discussion), and team projects, students can provide the support and insight to facilitate the achievement gains of others in a positive and helpful manner.

Acceptance and appreciation of student differences and diversity. Public schools today are being asked to respond to an increasingly diverse student population. According to the U.S. Department of Education's 1998 Civil Rights Survey, between 1976 and 1995 the race/ethnicity percentages within elementary and secondary schools shifted. The White, non-Hispanic population decreased by 11% during that time with the total minority population increasing by 11.1% (U.S. Department of Education, 1998). The most significant change has been the 7.1% increase in the Hispanic school population. According to the Center for Research on Education, Diversity, and Excellence (2000), the rapid demographic changes in the nation's population over the last three decades have impacted more on education than any other American social institution (U.S. Department of Education, 2000). Wittmer suggests that the term "minority" is rapidly losing significance in the nation's classrooms (1992). By the year 2056, the average U.S. citizen will trace their lineage to Africa, Asia, the Hispanic countries, the Pacific Islands, and almost anywhere other than Europe (Wittmer, 1992).

Most assuredly, diversity is more than a racial issue. The San Francisco Public Schools are promoting integration and enhancing student achievement without assigning students to schools based on race alone. Instead, they are basing placement on a diversity index that measures whether or not a student participates in public housing or free lunch programs, scored low on SAT tests, has a mother who finished high school, is proficient in English, previously attended a poorly performing school, or lives in a home where English is not the primary language. Many school officials are accepting the reality that celebrating diversity in its many forms must be embraced and must become a way of life.

Since the "I'm Black and I'm proud" era of the 1960s and early 1970s, many school officials have made greater efforts to educate all students on the accomplishments of all racial and cultural groups. Few can deny the continued importance of nonbiased instructional materials that augment racial and cultural pride and improved race relations. However, while many schools and school systems are moving in this direction, there is still significant resistance among some individual teachers and administrators. Controversy over implementation of an *Afrocentric Curriculum* reflects much of the resistance.

Many Black educators have long touted the benefits of the Afrocentric Curriculum in augmenting the understanding of all students on the great history of Africans and Black Americans who are of African descent. According to Samuel A. Iyewarun, the following benefits are most likely to accrue as a result of the implementation of the Afrocentric Curriculum in schools with large African American populations (1997, p. 12):

- Discipline is maintained.

- Values and high character are instilled.

- Dropout rates are lower.

- Academic achievement improves.

- Attendance at school and school-related activities improves.

- Motivation to succeed is greater.

- Youth are more likely to contribute to their communities and nations at large.

Certainly, the Afrocentric Curriculum is one way of increasing the amount of information taught in schools about African Americans (Iyewarun, 1997). More importantly, however, Iyewarun emphasizes that the Afrocentric Curriculum is a workable educational program to teach African American children "who are told who they are not!" (1997, p. 16). Asante (1994) notes that the Afrocentric Curriculum is an intellectual philosophy that views African Americans as agents or actors in the story of history rather than passive observers. Since it does not promote racism—only better understanding—it should be embraced if there is a desire for the benefits described by Iyewarun.

Those who criticize the Afrocentric Curriculum emphasize that it is a political rather than historical agenda and has little to do with factual reality. However, many of those who use it tout the same benefits identified by Iyewarun.

There is a need to enhance racial and cultural pride within some Black and Hispanic students. Yet the overriding need is to promote cultural and racial awareness among those outside of the race. Whether all students get the message through Afrocentrism or other multicultural offerings and activities, the teaching of tolerance must be an inherent component in effectively dealing with difference.

Freedom of student expression. Teachers must foster freedom of expression. When students feel uncomfortable about expressing themselves, they are more likely to disengage from the learning process. Teachers can encourage freedom by accepting various means of expression, by being willing to listen, and by showing emphatic understanding of and an interest in the child as a person.

While all students must learn how to express themselves in socially acceptable manners—for example, through the use of Standard English in speaking and writing—students should be encouraged to engage in various means of expression that may reflect individual or cultural strengths. For example, Black students who show what they feel is racial and cultural pride—such as the use of Black English when reading the poetry of Paul Laurence Dunbar, Maya Angelou, or other artists or musicians of a particular race or culture—should be encouraged, not "corrected."

If students get the message that teachers are unwilling to accept their cultural dialect or appearance, their racial pride, or listen to their concerns or responses, they are less likely to express themselves or bond with authority figures. Good teachers must create a climate in which all forms of expression are appreciated, particularly those that are unique to a particular race or culture.

Fostering a Climate of Acceptance and Understanding

Many underachieving students feel trapped in schools where teachers and administrators just don't understand them. Even though some teachers may not know what a child might be internalizing, experiencing, or feeling, teachers can still show a willingness to accept and validate the feelings of that child. Children, especially children of color, need to feel that perceived barriers to understanding can be eradicated. Otherwise, these students may continue to display the self-segregation that is unique for the oppositional identity they develop when they feel schools have been racist, unjust, and unfair. Teachers who differ from their students in race, gender, socioeconomic status, or lifestyle can still convey acceptance and understanding.

A teacher who shows a desire to understand and some sincerity in accepting student feelings can establish more meaningful bonds with the student. I advocate the use of *"feel, felt, found."* When students convey feelings of anger, frustration, or hopelessness, teachers can respond by saying, "I know how you *feel*," or "I can imagine how you must *feel*. I've been in situations where I *felt* the exact same way, but this is what I *found* out." The teacher can then share with the student insight on how to make the best of what appears to be a bad situation. Even when students are expressing feelings of victimization because of race, teachers who are racially different can still let them know, "I know how you *feel;* I may not have experienced exactly what you did because we differ in class and race, but I have *felt* injustices before, and this is what I *found* out."

Many students are alienated from schools because of the behavior of adults in the school environment who show no interest in the child or in anything the child feels is important. This simply means that other educators will have to reach out more because of the impact of those in the school who will not or cannot reach out enough.

Educators and school districts must remember that perceptions of the school by parents, students, and concerned citizens are often based on first impressions. In many cases, the physical appearance of the school and the "warmth" of the classroom determine those first impressions. The climate, therefore, has much to do with how parents, citizens, and students feel about the school, each classroom, and school personnel.

In creating a positive school and classroom climate, school officials are laying the foundation for a stronger home-school and community bond. Parents are more likely to feel good about schools and their officials when they realize that efforts are being made to recognize and enhance the unique nonacademic gifts of each child and provide each child with a safe school and classroom environment. Moreover, teachers who show compassion and understanding to students are more likely to engage in behavior with parents that also reflects their understanding, sincerity, concern, and compassion. Thus, the school climate can either enhance or diminish the positive relationships all school officials should want to develop with parents, citizens, and the community.

Chapter 8

Strengthening the Home-School Bond

In spite of the difficulties that family-school partnerships may entail, working together is critically important for students.

—Anne T. Henderson, Carl L. Marburger,
and Theodora Oams (1989)

The positive impact of parental involvement on the achievement motivation of students was documented in research performed by the National Committee for Citizens in Education in 1975. Anne Henderson reached the same conclusions in her 1987 book titled *The Evidence Continues to Grow: Parent Involvement Improves Student Achievement.*

More recently, in a 1997 national study on parental involvement commissioned by the National Center for Education Statistics, it was found that children do better in school when their parents (especially their fathers) are involved with their schools—whether their fathers live with them or not (Nord, 1997). The study looked at four types of school activities for parental involvement: attending a general school meeting; attending a regularly scheduled parent-teacher conference; attending a school or class event, and volunteering at the school. The study controlled four other factors that have been traditionally associated with a child's school success—race, ethnicity, parent's education, and family income—and found that:

- Children with involved fathers who live in two-parent families are more likely to get mostly A's, regardless of the level of the mother's involvement.

- Children who live in single-parent families headed by fathers are twice as likely to get mostly A's if their fathers are highly involved at school, compared to those whose fathers have little involvement (none or in only one school activity).

- While non-custodial fathers are less likely to participate at school than custodial fathers (only 31% participate in any school activity), when they are involved, they make a difference, particularly for children in grades six and above. Their children are much more likely to get A's, enjoy school, participate in extracurricular activities, and are less likely to repeat a grade.

- In single-parent families, children living with single fathers or single mothers are about equally likely to have highly involved parents, 46% and 49% respectively. When fathers have primary responsibility for raising their children, they are almost as involved in school activities as mothers in either two- or single-parent families. And the involvement of single parents—both mothers and fathers—is similar to that of mothers in two-parent families.

- Families with high parental involvement in their children's schools are more likely to visit a library, museum, or historical site with their children, and are more likely to have educational expectations for their children.

More importantly, however, the study found that mothers and fathers are more likely to be highly involved in their children's schools if the schools welcome parental involvement and make it easier for parents to be involved. The powerful positive impact of parental involvement was again documented by Henderson and Mapp (2002) in a report titled "A New Wave of Evidence: The Impact of School, Family, and Community Connections on Student Achievement." Yet as vital as parental involvement is to student achievement, as important as it is for schools themselves, many parents do much less than they should, and many schools engage in practices that limit parental involvement in school decision-making.

Indeed, the partnership between home and school is so very important that educators and administrators must take immediate steps to strengthen it. Schools must involve more Black and Hispanic parents, keep these parents excited, and use and strengthen other community resources and social systems that affect student development. Although many school officials seek to limit parental involvement to efforts within the home to foster achievement gains in children, evidence shows that parents can be educated to play significant roles in the school decision-making process (Kuykendall, 1977). Therefore, this chapter will address:

- Parental involvement (what it is and should be)

- Involving Black and Hispanic parents

- Keeping Black and Hispanic parents excited

- Using and strengthening other community resources and social systems

Parental Involvement

The term "parental involvement" means different things to different people. When I was director of the Citizens' Training Institute (CTI) of the National Committee for Citizens in Education (1975–78), I found that the answer to that question varied widely depending on the respondent. Of the 8,000 plus parents and community activists who each spent 3 to 4 days in monthly training retreats, over 90% of parents interviewed felt parental involvement meant collaboration with school officials with regard to school decisions on such things as curriculum, discipline codes, staffing, use of some educational materials, school uniforms, playground equipment, and extracurricular activities. Through the CTI, parents were trained to be effective partners in the education of their children. Many of those parents were so inspired, informed, encouraged, and empowered that they have since become school board members, city council representatives, and educators.

Many school officials are now starting to realize that parental involvement means more than helping the child at home. Schools can help parents gain the insight and understanding needed to be advocates for their children's school success and provide forums where they can learn more about effective parenting and what school officials want and need from them. While schools must encourage parents to help children with homework and develop good manners and discipline, they must also encourage parents to give children good and nourishing breakfasts, keep them inspired, read to them, and talk to them. It is abundantly clear, however, that the involvement of Black and Hispanic parents must include more than PTA membership, bake sales, and at-home assistance. Educators also must involve parents as:

- Classroom tutors, helpers, and field-trip volunteers
- Members of a local school decision-making team
- Members of the school district's salary committee
- Members of the school district's curriculum development committee
- Members of the district's disciplinary committee
- Members of the principal selection committee
- Members of the school or district budget committee
- Members of a school design committee
- Participants in teacher contract negotiations

Some states actually have legislation that calls for parental involvement in some of these areas. School officials will quickly discover what researchers have already discovered: involvement by Black and Hispanic parents usually results in improved student achievement (National Center for Education Statistics, 1997).

Once school officials expand their definition of what constitutes effective parental involvement, they can develop strategies that will involve parents at every conceivable level. However, involving Black and Hispanic parents requires more than an expanded definition of the term. School officials must also carefully develop strategies for getting and keeping parents excited about the school process, especially those parents who live far away from the child's desegregated school or those who have never been involved before.

Educators first must believe that the involvement of Black and Hispanic parents is of paramount importance. If school officials really believe that schools will benefit from parental involvement, they will take the necessary steps to make certain that extensive involvement does, in fact, occur.

Involving Black and Hispanic Parents

Many Black and Hispanic parents are likely to be more involved in school activities when their children are in the preschool and primary grades. Pre-primary education is on the rise for Black and Hispanic youth. Black children have traditionally enrolled in pre-primary education programs at higher rates than White and Hispanic children. In 1999, 73% of Black children ages 3–5 attended such programs, compared to 60% of White children, and 44% of Hispanic children (National Center for Education Statistics, 2001). Participation in pre-primary education programs such as Head Start, Nursery School, or Pre-Kindergarten help children prepare for elementary school. Even though pre-primary education programs also serve as childcare for working parents, they usually require parental involvement and support at some level, beyond the financial obligation.

Between 1991 and 1999, the percentage of children ages 3–5 who had attended center-based early childhood care and education programs but who had not yet entered kindergarten rose from 53% to 60%. The participation of children living in poverty increased from 44% to 52% (National Center for Education Statistics, 2001). This means that an increasing number of Black, Hispanic, and poor parents are aware of the expectation for parental support and involvement in the early stages of their children's education. Despite their involvement in the early stages of their children's education, many Black,

Hispanic, and poor parents are less likely to be encouraged to be as involved in the later grades as they were in the pre-primary and primary grades. While researching why Black children fail, Morgan (1980) emphasized that school officials must make the schools more inviting and solicitous of parental support because an intense level of involvement is needed in the intermediate grades, where the classroom environment is less socially interactive and more competitive and individualistic.

In previous chapters, we discussed the drop in self-image among Black youth between first and fifth grades. Some observers have even expressed alarm over a "fourth grade failure syndrome" among Black boys (Morgan, 1980). Parental involvement of Black and Hispanic parents during this critical stage in the development of their children is especially important. While I have not seen hard data suggesting that parental involvement in grades 4–7 would enhance self-image in Black students and end the fourth-grade failure syndrome, I find it interesting that research does show parents are less likely to be as involved in their children's education after third grade (Henderson, 1987). When one considers the possible impact of the fourth-grade failure syndrome, the need for more parental involvement at this grade level becomes obvious, for there appears to be a direct correlation. The more involved parents are in their children's education after third grade, the less likely these youth are to fail.

Teachers and administrators must assume a greater professional responsibility by actively enlisting parental involvement at every grade level so that this fourth-grade failure syndrome can be avoided and self-image can be enhanced, not damaged, as children grow older. The following are suggestions of what good teachers and administrators can do to encourage the participation of Black and Hispanic parents.

Maintain a Positive Attitude

To enlist parental support, teachers and administrators should make certain that their attitude is positive. Many Black and Hispanic parents to whom I've spoken have expressed dismay over the condescending and pedantic tones of some classroom teachers. It is important that educators refrain from using demeaning and degrading words to describe family structures. Terms such as "dysfunctional families" suggest to some Black and Hispanic students and parents that their family is inferior. Such words also convey a reluctance to accept the inherent strengths of families in diverse cultures.

Some educators would be surprised to learn of the tremendous strength that exists in many non-nuclear, but extended, Black and Hispanic families. Many single-parent families among Blacks and Hispanics are still supported by an extended network so that single mothers are not raising children alone (Morgan, 1980). The continued use of terms that reflect institutionalized disrespect for Black and Hispanic lifestyles only fosters alienation. Once teachers are able to see Black, Hispanic, and poor parents as capable individuals who deserve respect, they are more likely to make the overtures necessary to enhance the home-school partnership.

Make the First Contact Positive

Educators must make the first contact with the parent a positive one. Some parents may still harbor memories of their own negative school experiences and a few teachers they felt were demeaning and disrespectful. Many of these parents may hope for the best even though they actually fear for their own children.

Figure 8.1

Sample First Contact With Parent

Hello, I'd like to speak to the parent or guardian of
(Child's Name)_____.

I am so glad to have a chance to talk to you.
I am _____(Your Name)_____, your child's
_____(Grade or Subject)_____ teacher. I know
you're probably busy. I just wanted to take these few
minutes to let you know how delighted I am to have
(Child's Name)_____ in my class. Already I have
noticed his/her
_____(Strength)_____, his/her
_____(Strength)_____, and
his/her _____(Strength)_____. I am
looking forward to meeting you so that we can
discuss how we might work together to bring out
the very best in _____(Child's Name)_____.

Rather than first making contact with the home when the student has done something wrong, teachers should call parents early in the school year to share some good news and favorable anticipation. The suggested conversation presented in Figure 8.1 will take only a few minutes, but it can strengthen the parents' resolve to work closely with the school.

Many parents will be shocked to receive such a positive call from an obviously sincere and caring teacher. Some will get off the phone and turn to their child to let him or her know that this teacher is not to be given a hard time. I have had teachers who have tried this conversation report to me that many parents have cried because they were so moved by the teacher's show of concern.

During the first face-to-face visit with the parent, teachers should discuss the individual strengths and interests of the child. They should also seek to discern any sensitivities or special qualities that a child may have. The following questions illustrate how the teacher can learn more about the student and make the parents active participants in shaping how the teacher views and values their child:

- "What have you noticed about Kahlil that you consider outstanding?"

- "What kinds of things does Rasheki like doing the most?"

- "What activities do you and Luisa engage in at home?"

- "How many siblings are there to help Manuel at home?"

- "What has been Eli's previous experience with school?"

- "What kind of personality does Ellen show at home?"

- "Are there any talents Maria has that I should help her develop?"

- "Are there any nicknames Kashif has that I should know?"

- "What goals has José shared with you?"

- "How does Marquette get along with his friends outside of school?"

- "Are there any dietary considerations I should know about Zawadi?"

- "Does Yahri's name have a meaning I should understand?"

- "Who are LaShawn's favorite cartoon or storybook characters?"

- "What has Tiffany shared with you about her feelings about this school?"

- "Have there been any changes within Brandon's family that I should know about?"

If school officials do not show parents that they have a genuine interest in their children, many Black, Hispanic, and poor parents will assume the worst. The excessive suspensions, failures, and placements of Black youth, especially boys, in special education classes support the belief held by many Black parents that there is a conspiracy to destroy Black boys (Kunjufu, 1985). Some teachers may inadvertently advance that belief when they do not build on the strengths of their Black and Hispanic students. It is the teachers' identification and acceptance of these strengths that can arouse the desire of some parents to build meaningful and cooperative relationships with school personnel. Keep in mind that many Black and Hispanic parents are dealing with the day-to-day reality of their own survival. Some will avoid contact with the school if such contact brings only more bad news.

After primary contact is made, teachers can maintain contact with parents through notes or calls—especially when there is more good news to report. Teachers also should constantly remind parents that they are welcome partners and worthy of the school's utmost respect.

Be Consistently Positive

Some teachers say positive things about students when they talk to parents but maintain a negative attitude when interacting with the student during regular school hours. Some even write negative things in the child's cumulative folder after sharing positive things with parents. Eventually, parents will discover this hypocrisy, and it will make them more reluctant to establish meaningful relations with other school personnel.

Advocate for More Parent Education Classes in Your School or District

Parent education classes can be very helpful. There may be a big gulf between what the teacher expects of parents and what the parent feels is expected of him or her. Parent education classes can help parents understand such things as:

- How to develop positive values and character in children

- The school's mission, objectives, and rules

- How to develop a "home curriculum" that provides for after-school learning enrichment, more parent-student interaction, and discussion of school obstacles and milestones (Walberg, 1984)

- What the school expects of both parent and child, and what the school is offering in return

- What the parents' recourse is if their child is suspended, placed in special education, or disciplined unfairly

- Who the key players in the school are (such as the assistant principal, nurse, librarian, and coach)

Parent education classes can also give parents a better understanding of things they can do at home to enhance the motivation of their children. In my inspirational booklet, "You and Yours: Making the Most of This School Year" (1987), I share with parents and school officials the following 12 monthly activities centered around themes that can be used to improve parental involvement and student achievement:

1. **Dreaming of a better tomorrow**—Have parents work with children to set short- and long-term goals. Short-term goals can be things the student will accomplish within the day, the week, or month (such as, I will read two books this month). Long-term goals should reflect things the student will accomplish over a period of years—or by the time they are 25 years old (see the Success Chart in chapter 5, page 120).

2. **Each one-teach one**—Encourage parents to use older siblings (or relatives) as tutors or mentors for younger children.

3. **Staying on track**—Teach parents how to keep their children focused in the midst of peer and community distractions. Some students will want to do things other students are allowed to do—even if it means neglecting their studies or homework assignments. Teachers can discuss with parents the importance of getting students to determine what their priorities should be. If you've already had students complete the "Help/Hinder" activity included in the Success Chart in chapter 5, parents should be advised to conduct the same activity at home with their children. Many youth can remain focused when they understand that many activities they enjoy (parties, sports, recreation, talking on the phone, and so on) are enjoyed the most when they do

not prevent youth from studying, doing homework, or growing academically. When I was growing up, there was always something happening in the streets that made me want to be outside. Yet my parents forbade all social activities until after homework was completed. I was constantly reminded in my later grades that I was going to college and had to stay focused on getting better grades so I would receive scholarships.

4. **Taking tests**—Teach parents what to do to prepare their children not just for school exams but other "tests" they will encounter throughout their lives. Children will be tested to say "no" to drugs, to walk away from violent confrontations with others, and to persist in the face of setbacks.

5. **Making use of children's talents**—Teach parents to identify and build on the unique gifts, talents, and strengths of their own children.

6. **Learning never ends**—Help parents use home activities to keep children excited about learning (for example, children could help with cooking or learn to plant, prune, or decorate).

7. **Learning how to help others**—Parents should be taught to involve their children in charitable and community service endeavors.

8. **Being prepared**—Parents should teach their children the value of being prepared for school by making certain that children have all their necessary supplies and immunizations. School officials may have to provide assistance to poor parents or language-challenged parents to obtain supplies and the required shots.

9. **Completing homework**—Parents may not be able to help with homework because of their own limited educations, but they can be encouraged to create an atmosphere at home where students can quietly and successfully complete homework.

10. **The importance of punctuality**—Parents can be taught to get students to school on time. If this is a concern, school officials should invite parents to parenting workshops where time-management advice and other tips are shared. School officials may also be surprised to learn that many parents get their children out of the house in plenty of time to get to school. Children who are still chronically tardy may be responding to their discomfort in a particular class, feelings of under-appreciation or dislike from the teacher, taunting from other students, poor school and classroom climate, or even lack of school success. Remember, when the soul doesn't want to be in school, it's hard to get there on time.

11. **Get to know the school**—School officials should teach parents as much as they can about how the school works and encourage them to form partnerships as decision-makers.

12. **Use TV, radio, and mass media to your advantage**—Parents must be informed that just as school officials are using outside influences (such as TV, music, and movies) to teach children, they too can use these influences to teach their children right from wrong and how to respect the other gender, as well as people of other races and cultures. When music demeans and disrespects women, for example, parents can discuss

with their children why those lyrics are wrong and what the child's appropriate behavior should be.

School officials must remember to express school information in terms that parents can understand. Avoid the use of educational jargon, long words, and complex sentences (Massachusetts Advocacy Center, 1975). Sharing information builds trust and strengthens the home-school bond. Make sure your school isn't guilty of turning away those parent partners so necessary for school success.

Plan a "Family Fun Night" at Your School

A Family Fun Night involves all students and their families in entertainment and fun activities. This special night should be well advertised. I recommend calling it a "Family Fun Night" if you can provide games, clowns, or other forms of entertainment. Movies or videos may be shown to small children to keep them occupied, while older children and parents engage in other activities. Contact parents through flyers and by telephone. Prizes can be awarded to classrooms that have the best parent attendance. This night should be a celebration of everything that makes the school and its students, the parents, and the community so unique and special.

School officials should involve the entire school community in Family Fun Night. Local businesses can be asked to provide prizes for raffles and other awards. Similarly, administrators and employees from local recreation centers, city government officials, and civic and social leaders can also be invited to make this special night a celebration of the community as a family. Call upon local radio stations to advertise and encourage parents, concerned citizens, and community leaders to unite around school activities that will enhance student motivation and achievement.

Encourage Parents to Join Groups and Organizations

Another successful way to involve parents is to encourage them to join established parent/citizen groups or to start their own organizations. Many Black, Hispanic, and poor parents can benefit tremendously from organized involvement with other parents in the school. Established parent/citizen groups can monitor school activities and facilitate overall school improvement. Once school officials have involved parents, it is important to maintain the parents' excitement and participation. For many educators, however, sustaining parental involvement and support is easier said than done.

Keeping Black and Hispanic Parents Excited

There are several explanations for waning excitement and involvement of some Black and Hispanic parents at intermediate, junior high, and high school levels. All too often, parents lose interest because their children have lost interest.

I know of numerous parents who see some schools as insensitive, disinterested, punitive, and uncommitted. One parent, whose child had a B average until he reached junior high school, lamented, "It's almost as though they just don't want to see him make it." I don't believe the majority of schools are this way. Yet it is important that educators don't create an appearance of indifference. The steps outlined previously for establishing a more conducive school and classroom climate and meeting student needs will thwart such an appearance of indifference.

There may be logistical barriers that keep parents from maintaining their involvement in their children's schools. For many Black and Hispanic parents, transportation and child-care are obstacles. If a child is bused to a school far from his or her neighborhood, it may be extremely difficult for parents to take part in school functions or to be a visible presence in the schools. Administrators and teachers must take steps to provide transportation, or they must meet the parent halfway. Also, school functions for parents should encourage family participation. Activities can be planned in kindergarten classrooms for smaller children, while parents and older children can visit classrooms and take part in other activities. Childcare should not be a factor in maintaining parent support.

The scheduling of school activities is also a concern. In some neighborhoods where there is high unemployment (leaving many parents at home during the day), high crime, and poorly lit streets, it may be advisable to have some school functions during the day. Certainly, Saturday and evening events may be best for working parents. Through collaboration with parents and the community, teachers and school officials can determine appropriate times for school activities to be planned during the year.

If school officials exhibit more concern for students and follow many of the suggestions outlined in previous chapters, their schools will have more parent participation and support. However, good schools will go a step further by seeking to create a community of caring that involves the entire school community in facilitating student success.

Where language barriers exist, schools must make sure that materials sent home and available in the schools are translated into languages spoken by parents. Importantly, translators should be employed to attend teacher-parent conferences and school events.

When I wrote my first book, *Developing Leadership for Parent/Citizen Groups,* the publisher, the National Committee for Citizens in Education, had it printed in Spanish and English. Many school districts purchased copies of each book for distribution to parents. I was overjoyed by the numerous letters I received—most handwritten in Spanish—from grateful parents, many indicating that it was the first time they had been given anything from the school they could understand.

Using and Strengthening Community Resources and Social Systems

To paraphrase the English poet John Donne, no school is an island; all schools serve the interests of the communities in which they are located. For this reason, partnerships with the community improve school effectiveness. Unfortunately, some school officials see low-income communities as part of the problem. In an unpublished study I completed in 1986 titled "Counselor Attitudes Toward Delinquent Youth," I received responses from counselors in Howard, Prince George's, Dorchester, and Montgomery Counties in Maryland and Washington, DC. Many counselors blamed neighborhoods/communities for the delinquent behavior of their students. Those students coming from neighborhoods with high crime, unemployment, and high drug use were considered least likely to succeed. I am living proof that this does not have to be the case. An encouraging school official can have a positive influence on a student—regardless of community blight.

There are many appropriate resources within all communities that can be harnessed and used effectively to augment student achievement and school improvement. Educators can make best use of community resources by:

- Creating "Blue Ribbon" community panels

- Recruiting and using community businesses

- Making use of other social systems in the community

- Sharing insight on how to revise discipline codes

- Sharing insight on other community agencies and resources

- Providing feedback on planned school functions and activities

- Sharing insight on other challenges facing the community so all can be effective trouble-shooters

- Featuring a school "Wall of Fame" where accomplished community leaders and former graduates are featured and acknowledged

- Showing a united commitment to the success of every child in the school

Through outreach with the community, administrators and teachers can identify role models and mentors within the school community who can work with students to keep them motivated. As school officials seek to involve community leaders and resources in the school, they must also work collaboratively with agencies and institutions that serve the interest of families and children (Clinton, 1996).

Recruit Community Role Models and Mentors

All concerned citizens should share the job of educating youth. Every community has residents who can be exemplary role models to youth. School leaders can take the initiative in reaching out to these potential mentors and providing opportunities for them to influence and guide youth in schools and classrooms.

Our Black and Hispanic male youth are in particular need of strong role models who can help them see themselves in the most positive light. Schoolteachers in this country are overwhelmingly White, middle-class, and female. The pool of Black and Hispanic male teachers is dwindling. According to the U.S. Department of Education's National Center for Education Statistics (1997), all 50 states have launched measures to recruit and retain Black male teachers (National Education Association, 2003).

Kenneth Jones (1986) found that as Black males approach early adulthood, guidance from older Black men is critical. Good role models can offset negative realities or myths regarding the Black community (such as high unemployment, dropout rates, and inclinations toward antisocial behavior). Rather than leave the development of Black and Hispanic males solely to the schools, peer groups, or chance (Perkins, 1975), schools can respond to the needs of their male and female students for guidance by enlisting the support of volunteer mentors who will:

- Help youth become more responsible.

- Help youth set short- and long-term goals.

- Help youth correct behavior that can alter their lives.

- Help youth break down perceived and actual barriers to school success.

- Help students improve in academic areas where they are weakest.

- Improve youth discipline and motivation by being a real example of what can be done with a purpose and a plan.

- Help youth develop better bonds with others in the community so that as they become adults, they too will be able to "give something back" (Collins, Tamarkin, & Haley, 1990).

If they seek the assistance of respected role models in the community, school officials will discover there are some very committed individuals who will devote a few hours a week to developing personal bonds with students. As Akbar (1991) noted, this bond can facilitate a boy's journey into manhood.

Create Partnerships With Community Businesses

School officials must remember that businesses do have a stake in the education and the socialization of students. Businesses and other community institutions can be encouraged to:

- Provide resources (paper, school supplies, equipment, furniture, and so on).

- Have a representative serve as the school liaison who has a visible presence in the school on a weekly basis.

- Have a representative talk to a class or student body on how to succeed in business.

- Arrange for field trips to larger companies or industries within the city.

- Provide incentive rewards to students for good attendance, creativity, or improved achievement.

- Assist students or classes with special projects designed to improve math or business skills.

Create Partnerships With the Religious Community

School officials must be mindful of the tremendous roles religious institutions can play in the lives of Black and Hispanic families. It does not really matter whether or not students and their parents attend church regularly, school officials should acknowledge Black and Hispanic churches as community resources that can facilitate both effective parental involvement and student success.

In his thought-provoking and detailed study of African American families, Wallace Charles Smith (1985) notes that churches can be powerful resources for schools. Smith calls for:

- A cooperative effort between churches and schools whereby churches can create their own PTA chapters

- Development of more church-sponsored after-school programs with planned activities in the warm, friendly, and caring church environment

- Use of retired persons and senior citizens as volunteers in community tutorial programs sponsored by the church

Importantly, churches within Black and Hispanic communities can be encouraged by school officials to "adopt" local schools and provide adult volunteers to work with the respective school as volunteers in other capacities as well. As more churches develop their abilities to seek grant funding, school officials can work collaboratively with them to write proposals for long-term funding that can address sensitive school problems such as discipline, dropout, drug abuse, teen pregnancy, a lack of motivation to achieve, poor teacher attitudes, and other challenges unique to a school or community.

Other Social Systems in the Community

In addition to businesses, most communities have some kind of government-sponsored recreation center, Boys & Girls Clubs, and other family service agencies and institutions. School officials should make a list of resource organizations and institutions serving children in their school community and then contact the organizations to determine how they could help the school. These organizations may be able to identify mentors or share information on after-school programs that can serve the needs of children for constructive after-school activities. The ability of school officials to develop and maintain positive relations with community resources is very important if student achievement really is the desired outcome. Moreover, every effort must be made by school officials to involve as many businesses, community agencies, institutions, churches, and outreach centers as possible in their ongoing efforts to improve schools and foster individual student achievement (Henderson & Mapp, 2002).

The Marriage of Home and School

The one marriage which must work for the sake of the children is the marriage between home and school. School officials who work to improve parental involvement are sure to see significant gains in student achievement. There are so many ways to encourage parental involvement; educators must remain persistent. In some cases, training programs or workshops on effective parenting may be necessary to improve student success.

Surely, educating and preparing all students for life and school success in this society is not easy. However, effective use of community resources and other social systems will help tremendously. When schools make effective use of these home and community resources, children benefit. The importance of counselors and individual volunteers who can serve as mentors and *Merchants of Hope* cannot be ignored. More will be said of the power of these *Merchants of Hope* in the next chapter.

Chapter 9

The Power of Counselors, Mentors, and *Merchants of Hope*

You must become your brother's keeper, for if you're not, he'll drag you down in his ruins.

—W.E.B. DuBois, 1907

Everyone can be great because everyone can serve.

—Rev. Dr. Martin Luther King, Jr. (1968)

Anyone who enriches the life of another—on a short- or long-term basis—is a *Merchant of Hope.* It is my fervent belief that all concerned citizens—not just those employed by our schools—have meaningful roles they can play as *Merchants of Hope.* Certainly, it takes *everyone* to educate *everyone.* As more citizens unleash the potential power they hold as *Merchants of Hope,* fewer children will be left behind, more families will thrive, and our country will preserve its greatness.

When there is personal outreach, mentees and mentors alike experience the benefits. In interviews I've conducted with 200 mentors, counselors, "Big Brothers," "Big Sisters," tutors, and "Buddies," 100% of respondents indicated that their outreach endeavors made coping with their own life challenges much easier. All felt that the rewards of counseling and mentoring were priceless.

This chapter will explore the power of counseling and mentoring while offering suggestions to enhance the endeavors of those who serve in such capacities. Importantly, the power of *Merchants of Hope* will be analyzed as we look briefly at why the need for *Merchants of Hope* is so great, who can meet this need, what *Merchants of Hope* can do, and how *Merchants of Hope* can make a difference.

Why Do We Need More *Merchants of Hope*?

Even if we lived in a perfect world with perfect, functional families and homes, no crime, no violence, perfect transitions from school to college to work for everyone, no job loss, no stress, and no discernable hopelessness, we would still need *Merchants of Hope*. The bottom line is, even in the best of times, we still need each other.

My high school chemistry teacher often reminded our class of the findings of a Russian scientist who noted that humans were only using 15% of their brains. Mr. Oliver urged us to strive to be 85% better at anything we chose to do. Each of us can still strive for self-improvement and contribute to the betterment of our own families, schools, and communities. One of the things many basketball aficionados loved about former professional ball player Michael Jordan was his ability to make his teammates better. *Merchants of Hope* who work to enrich their communities similarly make others better because they help make so many situations better. Since ours is not a perfect world, the importance of caring, compassionate *Merchants of Hope* is magnified significantly.

Data show that Black and Hispanic youth need good counselors and mentors at every stage of their development and not just in elementary and high school. In a study of White, Black, and Hispanic students' transitions to a community college, Weissman (1998) not only found the transition process for Black and Hispanic youth to be more stressful, but also found that the grades Black and Hispanic students earned in the first semester at the study colleges were lower than the grades earned by White students with similar standardized test scores. This fact suggests that not only must faculty and staff at institutions of higher learning do more to ease this transition, but other adults who can serve as counselors and mentors must also offer intervention techniques. Considering the low retention rates for Black and Hispanic youth at 2- and 4-year colleges, more outreach and intervention are needed.

Nearly three-quarters (73.1%) of all college degrees awarded in 1996–97 were awarded to White students. Consider also that in 1997–98 (U.S. Department of Education, 2000):

- Blacks received 10% of all associate degrees awarded, 8.3% of all bachelor's, 7.7% of all master's, 5.4% of all doctoral, and 7.2% of all first professional degrees awarded.

- Hispanics received 7.7% of all associate degrees awarded, 5.5% of all bachelor's, 4.1% of all master's, 3.2% of all doctoral, and 4.6% of all first professional degrees awarded.

Much more can—and must—be done to increase the percentage of Blacks and Hispanics who obtain college and professional degrees. Counselors and mentors can offer valuable assistance in helping these students fulfill the dreams they have for prosperity through legitimate professional undertakings.

The challenges facing Black males in contemporary society have already been well documented. In its *State of Black America Report* (2000), the National Urban League found that structural changes in the labor market and discriminatory hiring practices have created wide gaps between the earnings of Black and White men with a disproportionate number of Black men living in poverty. Unemployment figures for Black males have been four times higher than for White males during various points in the 1990s (U.S. Census Bureau, 2000). The Sentencing Project, in its study of Black men and the criminal justice system, found that the figure representing Black men who were part of the criminal justice system (on trial, on parole, on probation, or in jail) was consistently nearly 40% higher than the figure representing those in higher education during the 1990s (Mauer, 1990).

Figures released in 2002 by the Bureau of Labor Statistics show that rising unemployment rates for Blacks and Hispanics threaten economic gains attained during the booming 1990s. In December 2001, the unemployment rate for Blacks was 10.2% and 7.9% for Hispanics while the national jobless rate for all workers was just 5.8%. According to Stephanie Armour in her assessment of current trends (2002), the following were cited as reasons for this persistent gap in employment:

- Educational disparities—Blacks and Hispanics are less likely to have high school or advanced degrees. Only 56% of Hispanics and 77% of Blacks have high school diplomas compared to 88% of Whites.

- Industry representation—Hispanics are now concentrated in low-paying jobs that many Blacks once held in the manufacturing, hotel, and restaurant service industries.

- Discrimination—Experts agree that hiring discrimination continues to put Blacks and Hispanics at a disadvantage.

All of these statistics simply underscore the tremendous need for good citizens, as *Merchants of Hope,* to reach out to Black and Hispanic youth. In serving as mentors and counselors, dedicated citizens can offset or eliminate altogether these disturbing trends that have the potential to negate all of the advances Blacks and Hispanics have made before the year 2000.

Who Can Be a Counselor or a Mentor?

Men and women who have received the professional training to be counselors understand that the art of counseling allows one to give professional guidance that often utilizes psychological methods, especially in collecting a case history. School guidance counselors often have extensive training in pupil personnel services, while school psychologists and social workers who are called upon to counsel students and families have received academic training in the behavioral sciences. Yet those who enter the field of counseling usually bring with them a strong desire to help others. The importance of the required academic preparation, training, and skill enhancement that improve the effectiveness of professional counselors should not be underestimated. However, without a corresponding desire to help, the ability to love the humanity in others, or a caring countenance, even academically prepared and professional counselors will be unable to reach needy youth and their families.

Anyone who cares enough about the future to touch other lives, anyone willing to build on a foundation of human compassion and concern to become a professional counselor will find the academic rigor gratifying and the experience of counseling highly satisfying. I have had the experience of speaking at numerous conferences for professional counselors (the National Conference of the American Association of Counseling Development and other state association conferences as well), and I have been moved by the competence of some very committed and courageous professionals to uplift and inspire.

Becoming a mentor is much easier in many ways. Who can become a mentor? Anyone who cares. There is a well-known spiritual hymn sung in many Black Protestant churches that says simply, "God uses ordinary people." Those *Merchants of Hope* who serve as mentors to others are often ordinary people—concerned men and women who find the inner fortitude to be of service. While mentoring doesn't require advanced degrees or educational preparation, mentoring effectiveness *can* be enhanced with training.

HOSTS Mentor Training

One of the most powerful mentoring programs in the nation was launched in 1971 when Bill Gibbons, a former teacher in Vancouver, Washington, founded the HOSTS Corporation (now named HOSTS Learning). The goal of HOSTS Learning since its inception has been to provide a research-based, structured mentoring framework that will, in the phrase that defines the HOSTS acronym, "Help One Student To Succeed." The program matches community volunteers, business partners, and student mentors with at-risk students to accelerate achievement in reading, language arts, Spanish, and math. HOSTS Learning trains over 100,000 mentors annually. A federal, multi-state impact study found that students in HOSTS programs produced consistent improvement in educational attainment at every grade level from one to nine (Cardenas & Chahin, 2000). An editorial in *USA Today* titled "Merging for Their Minds" (1999), indicated that HOSTS programs can begin producing results in months. This is because of the four powerful effects of this national program:

1. HOSTS transforms the schooling experience of children by increasing school attendance; making readers of nonreaders; achievers of underachievers; and confident, engaged learners of previously shy, isolated, and reticent learners.

2. For many students, the experience with HOSTS is life-changing. HOSTS substantially benefits students' social and emotional development, their sense of confidence and competence, and their attitude and outlook on learning.

3. HOSTS benefits mentors as well as students. Two populations of mentors appear to be most powerfully affected by HOSTS: residents of retirement communities (including the very elderly) and peer and high school student mentors.

4. HOSTS catalyzes and supports improvements in student learning and personal efficacy, teacher practice and satisfaction, campus climate and expectations, mentor and community connections, and overall school success that extend well beyond the HOSTS classroom.

Recognized by the Education Commission of the States and the U.S. Department of Education for its success, the

HOSTS program has served over a million students in 38 states, the District of Columbia, Puerto Rico, and El Salvador. The program has fostered strong partnerships with numerous corporations and businesses. In fact, the National Governors Association has touted the HOSTS Program. In 1997, then Governor Thomas R. Carper of Delaware became one of the most vocal proponents of mentoring. A HOSTS mentor himself, Governor Carper not only spent time one day a week tutoring a Black fifth grader at an elementary school in Wilmington, Delaware, he also led his state to spend $350,000 on mentoring programs in fiscal 1997. Other elected officials and "ordinary people" interested in becoming HOSTS volunteers can contact the company directly at 1-800-833-4678 or visit their website at www.hosts.com.

Unstructured Mentoring Programs

Although HOSTS Learning and other mentoring programs like it offer structured mentoring and have a proven track record of success, many unstructured mentoring programs have similar success. These programs also "help one student to succeed," even though they are not directly affiliated with the HOSTS corporation. For example, my sorority adopted a middle school in the District of Columbia. Fifteen sorority members asked the school principal for the opportunity to serve as mentors to 15 at-risk girls. I have found my mentoring experience to be almost as gratifying as teaching. Anyone and everyone who cares about kids will find mentoring a marvelous means of making an impact on more lives. Indeed, there are many more lives that can and must be touched. In order to be a mentor, one must only have the desire to spend a few hours a week assisting a youth in some aspect of professional growth. Proper training is not required.

There is so much you can do if you would like to be a mentor and you are looking for ways to make a difference in an unstructured mentoring program. Through programs such as HOSTS, America's Promise, Best Friends, Big Brothers Big Sisters, and others, children are being tutored, counseled, and encouraged. In addition, many corporations prepare employees to serve as tutors and mentors even without the extensive HOSTS preparation. Under the leadership of retired United States Air Force General Robert T. Herrera, USAA Insurance in San Antonio, Texas, matched over 600 mentoring employees with students in the city's public schools. Many churches throughout the country have launched similar mentoring programs that have helped mentees and mentors alike.

What Can *Merchants of Hope* Do?

Whether you are a professionally trained counselor or a mentor in a structured or unstructured program, you can be very effective. The following tips will help both counselors and mentors enhance the efficacy of their endeavors.

Build on Strengths

Every child will not earn a doctoral degree or become a physician. However, *Merchants of Hope* can help students focus on getting legitimate jobs. Counselors and mentors who help students develop their nonacademic strengths will certainly enhance their confidence and self-esteem through academics. They will then be able to help students focus on career choices that magnify their strengths.

Help Students Cope With the Challenges of Today's Troubled Times

Those of us who have made it to adulthood know it's not easy being a child or teenager. The lives of many children and teens involve violence on many levels, and adults are not doing enough to prevent youth violence. In commentary shared in 2001 in *USA Today,* Marian Wright Edelman, founder and president of the Children's Defense Fund, faulted adults who teach children that violence is the way to solve disputes. Edelman noted that instead of focusing on preventive measures—giving children the early guidance, attention, and moral foundation they need—we wait until lives are destroyed and then we respond by imposing increasingly harsh punishments. Counselors and mentors can help youth with decisions related to:

- **Schoolwork**—The more confidence students develop in completing school work, the more focused and determined they will become. Mentors who assist in this regard give students a monumental lift.

- **Home challenges**—Many Black and Hispanic youth who are having challenges with parents or with their home situations can benefit from listening to the advice and counsel of other concerned adults.

- **Peer pressure**—Remember the needs students have for affection, appreciation, and achievement. When adults counsel and mentor youth, they must help them focus on the future and how their actions today will impact their lives tomorrow. An understanding of the effects of institutional and individual racism on Black and Hispanic students and the development of the oppositional identity in many of these youth will help adults in their efforts to help youth who feel tempted to do the wrong things as a result of their association with frustrated, alienated peers.

- **Dating**—Many young people don't know how to treat members of the opposite sex because they have never been taught how. Adults can give advice on dating do's and don'ts. Even with what is perceived as a generation gap, adults can help youth understand appropriate behavior. Adult men and women are needed to advise youth—as early as possible—on when and how to be good dating partners. Importantly, teen girls who are in abusive dating relationships should be counseled so they do not continue to accept physical abuse at the present time or when they become adult women.

- **Sex**—Counselors and mentors who develop rapport with youth are likely to be asked for advice with regard to sexual development and activities. When I was a counselor, many students shared with me their frustration over the sexual advances of other students. A proponent of abstinence before marriage, I have encouraged this behavior in all of those who sought my advice. Adults must remember that student focus should be on the future. Young women who want to complete their educations reduce their chances when teenage sexual promiscuity leads to unplanned pregnancy. Similarly, young men should be advised that making babies or "getting over" on naive girls does not constitute manhood.

- **Drugs**—Sometimes it is hard to "just say no," but adults should be prepared to share with youth the perils, pitfalls, and punishments for drug abuse. We can ill afford to risk the destruction of more young lives through drug, alcohol, and tobacco abuse.

- **Jobs**—Many youth are challenged to find and keep decent jobs. Adults can help youth find jobs and develop the job etiquette (for example, how to dress, interview, and conduct themselves) that will help them to stay employed.

- **College**—Many Black and Hispanic youth who want to go to college need adults who can help them with the admissions process. Had it not been for the counselors and mentors I had who helped me complete forms, including the financial statements my parents had to complete, I never would have made it to college with four scholarships.

- **Future**—Hindsight is 20/20. Too many children and teens can't focus on the future because they think of it as too far away. Adults must help students understand that the future is now. I'll never forget the words I received from one adult mentor who told me, "If you studied a third as much time as you spend jumping double Dutch, you'd be a genius." She helped me focus on my future at a time when all I wanted was an enjoyable here and now. Youth must have seeds for future greatness planted very early in their lives.

- **Recidivism**—With the growing number of incarcerations among Black and Hispanic youth (girls included), more *Merchants of Hope* will be needed to help ex-convicts lead meaningful lives. Recidivism is a relapse into criminal behavior or previous bad habits that could lead to re-incarceration. Parole officers and probation officers play critical roles in keeping youthful offenders out of trouble, but they need concerned citizens and communities to help prepare those who have been incarcerated to live crime-free lives. Importantly, many ex-convicts simply need new associations so they will not fall back into unproductive behavior patterns.

Be Unbiased

I have heard many horror stories of counselors who have urged Black and Hispanic students to seek menial, low paying positions rather than professional careers. Counselors and those who serve as mentors should use the Success Chart from chapter 5 (page 120) to help students reach their goals and should avoid negative comments about students and their chances for success in legitimate fields or career choices.

How Can *Merchants of Hope* Make a Difference?

Now that you know why we need adults and teens to serve as counselors and mentors and you are well aware that anyone can serve, it is important that you understand how to do those things counselors and mentors can do best.

Listen, Listen, Listen

Each of us has two ears and one mouth for a reason. The more we listen to our youth, the more we bond with them and the more meaningful our advice to them will be.

Allow Job Shadowing

A poll conducted by Junior Achievement in January 2002 found that many students had unrealistic expectations in regards to finding their ideal job, salary potential, and likelihood of working in their chosen career ("Survey of America's . . . ," 2002). Job shadowing is an experience that has become increasingly important for students because it provides real on-the-job experiences and allows them to learn much more about possible career choices and the workplace environment.

Counselors and mentors can match students with other adults who are willing to be shadowed, or they can serve in this capacity themselves. Annual Job Shadow Day is on February 2, although this activity can continue throughout the school year.

Watch for Early Warning Signs of Trouble

While I do not believe negative labeling is effective, I do believe that when adults see warning signs, they should intervene in helping students understand how to behave appropriately. For example, if a student appears angry and distraught constantly, it could be a sign of fear, frustration, or abuse of some kind. Counseling and/or therapy might then be an appropriate intervention strategy. At one time I counseled potential high-school dropouts in a program called Youth Consultation Services (YCS) in Newark, New Jersey. Teenagers were sent by their high schools to YCS for counseling, educational enrichment, cultural development, and tutoring. Those teenagers selected had shown warning signs of dropout, which included chronic class cutting and absences, anger, lack of motivation to succeed in school, poor school performance, and apparent hopelessness. During the time they spent at YCS, these youths were taught and inspired to reach legitimate goals. When educators see certain negative behaviors in youth, rather than victimize the student, they should attempt to resocialize that student. We can turn negative behaviors into positive growth; however, this can only happen when educators, parents, and *Merchants of Hope* pay attention to the mood swings, frustrations, and fears of youth who may be crying out through inappropriate behavior for help. All behavior is learned, and children must also be taught to respect human life and to behave appropriately when others confront and disrespect them. Training in peer mediation and conflict resolution has been proven effective in diminishing behavior problems in youth who have shown a propensity for violence in previous encounters (Scott, 2003).

Teach Children to Mediate and Manage Anger

Adults can turn off violent TV programming, or if they know children have been watching violence on TV or listening to violent music, they can engage children in discussions about the content. Whenever my teenage daughters wanted to watch programs I knew had violent content, I would always make them write short paragraphs after viewing these programs. In these paragraphs, they were required to share their feelings on the violent content they witnessed and what could have been done or said differently in that program or movie. With my current mentee (who I've had since she was 12), I discuss violent lyrics in rap music and violence on television in my attempts to teach her appropriate behavior and to socialize her. I understand that her outlook on life and her feelings about right and wrong are affected by her prior socialization. Children can be re-socialized. They can be taught to manage anger. Teachers and peer mediators can teach youth to manage their anger by implementing the following tips:

- Ask the angered parties to discuss the specific action or event that caused the anger.

- Discuss whether there was an intentional aggravation on the part of another. If yes, why? How did the behavior exacerbate or escalate the problem?

- Ask each angry person to pretend to be the other person and share what they would have, could have, or should have done differently.

- Ask angry students to list the pros and cons of the following:

  - Holding grudges

  - Retaliating

- Being angry

- Making up

- Moving past or dealing with differences

- Using the energy exerted by being angry to promote physical health

- Mediating disputes

My mentee was in a constant state of anger: angry with her mother, her teachers, family members—everyone she felt had been unkind or unfair to her. It was important for me to help her to understand that anger was debilitating and unhealthy. I was able to help her to manage her anger when and where it occurred by helping her stay focused on the BIG picture—her future and her improved achievement. As long as she understood where she was going, she could appreciate the fact that responding or giving in to anger could thwart her chances of having the future she knew she wanted and—I convinced her—that she deserved.

Magnifying Your Power

As a *Merchant of Hope,* take time now to magnify the power of your outreach by using the tips in this chapter. It doesn't matter if you devote 2 hours or 20 minutes a week to a child. Any amount of time will make a difference—if you're willing to make the effort.

You can also be a *Merchant of Hope* to other adults, including co-workers, friends, and family members. I have been especially encouraged by the way corporations, government agencies, school districts, and local schools have instituted mentoring programs between veteran employees and newer professionals. School districts nationwide have fostered informal mentoring relationships that pair new teachers with wise veteran mentors who provide tips and encouragement.

During the year 2001, lawmakers in the Commonwealth of Virginia made teacher mentoring mandatory for beginning teachers and teachers new to that state. While the state of Maryland has no statewide requirement, the state created a $5 million grant program in 2001 aimed at expanding mentoring programs between new and veteran teachers—especially in schools with a high number of new teachers or disadvantaged students. A study by the National Center for Education Statistics shows that 20% of new teachers leave the profession in the first 3 years. In urban districts this figure can be as high as 30 to 50%. However, there is evidence that mentoring makes new teachers feel better about their profession. A study by the National Center for Education Statistics found that 70% of teachers who met with a mentor once a week said their instructional skills improved "a lot" because of the contact (Samuels, 2000).

Holloman found that mentoring between teachers was one way of retaining and recruiting more minority teachers. Black teachers are approximately 8% of the teaching staffs in public schools and Hispanics comprise 3% (Holloman, 2002). When paired with more experienced mentors, new minority teacher recruits experienced more success in preparation and classroom activities. Importantly, teacher-student relations improve when teachers who have benefited as mentees are able to facilitate career development in high school students through teacher-student mentoring (Tonoli, 2001). Whether mentoring is teacher to teacher or teacher to student, it ultimately enhances teacher and student performance.

When adults mentor other adults, they create opportunities for long-term institutional success. I urge such partnerships in every work environment. Importantly, many schools and universities have also found the power of mentoring is magnified when incoming freshmen are paired with upperclassmen who can serve as mentors or Pals. The PALS Program at Howard University in Washington, DC, has become legendary for the impact it has had on the motivation of incoming freshmen who are encouraged to succeed and accomplish more than their exemplary upper-class mentors.

To magnify your power as a mentor, counselor, or *Merchant of Hope,* you must:

- See yourself as a unique winner capable of working wonders.

- Identify your own nonacademic strengths and use them to your benefit.

- Manage your time more effectively. Remember, it's how you use the 24 hours you get each day that determines what you get out of life.

- Remember that you are a blessing for someone, so you must see yourself as "too blessed to be stressed" (Cook, 1998).

- Seek the advice and counsel of people who can mentor you.

- Not be discouraged when your outreach doesn't appear to be appreciated.

- Not become frustrated—there are others who will respond to your overtures. You may not be able to reach everyone you would like to reach.

- Give first to your family and then to the families of others.

Filling the Need

There is a tremendous need for *Merchants of Hope* outside of schools (concerned citizens, volunteers, business, civic, social, community, and religious leaders) to participate in the growth, development, and education of youth who are at risk for failure in school or life—especially those who are Black and Hispanic. This chapter has shown that there is much that *Merchants of Hope* can do to change lives for the better. However, many people who would like to make a difference in young lives may not know how to proceed in becoming school volunteers, tutors, and mentors, particularly if they do not have school-aged children. Therefore, school leaders must make others aware of the need schools have for their involvement and the many ways they can make a difference. Importantly, school leaders must have an action plan to make the best use of the power residing in these community partners. More will be said about expanding school leadership outside of the school building in the next chapter.

Chapter 10

School Leadership

The fastest way to fail is to improve on yesterday's successes.

—W. Edwards Deming (cited in Easum, 1993)

In presentations made to school officials and corporate executives, I have often emphasized that, more than anything else, *leadership is a process for promoting change.* All too often corporate executives, school policy makers, and managers who are reluctant (or afraid) to change just maintain the status quo. It takes a committed visionary and valiant crusader to navigate the vicissitudes of change in any corporation, organization, agency, institution, or bureaucracy. Real leaders—regardless of title, position, status, or situation—understand that change is constant. Therefore, effective leaders must adapt and educate others on how best to implement improvements and bring about required changes. Change is sometimes difficult. I believe school leaders must have the patience of Job, the wisdom of Solomon, and the agility of a tight rope walker in order to bring about school improvement and necessary change. As effective school leaders, school officials must always seek ways to serve and to meet the changing needs of children and parents who are school consumers.

In fact, a leader is anyone who is realistic about the need for change, anyone who accepts his or her responsibility to facilitate change and foster improvement, and anyone who helps others overcome a resistance to change. People who want things to remain the same are prone to make excuses for their inertia. The feature box below lists popular excuses for resisting new ideas and precluding requisite change. School officials and leaders should also remember the seven last words of any dying institution: "We never did it that way before" (Southerland, 1999).

Twenty Excuses People Use to Resist Change

1. "My problem is different."
2. "These kids can't be helped."
3. "It just won't work."
4. "I've tried that before."
5. "That's not my problem."
6. "This is almost the same as what I'm doing."
7. "I had the same idea 10 years ago."
8. "There's not enough time."
9. "I don't have the authority."
10. "I don't have enough help."
11. "I don't have the training."
12. "It's too impractical."
13. "What if it fails?"
14. "It's too complicated."
15. "We're already inundated."
16. "It's a good idea, but . . ."
17. "No one else wants to."
18. "Let's be realistic."
19. "This too shall pass."
20. "You can't teach an old dog new tricks."

This chapter has been added because I believe that school officials and leaders must clarify and embrace their roles and responsibilities so as to facilitate school improvement and reform. Those leaders willing to take risks to remedy education and change the status quo will be rejuvenated by their endeavors. This chapter will:

- Help leaders face the future as facilitators of change.

- Provide a framework for leading in an ever-changing society.

- Review the roles and responsibilities of school leaders.

- Present recommendations for school reform.

Facing the Future as Facilitators of Change

In his analysis of societal trends and transitions, William Easum noted that two kinds of leadership surface in every period of transition. First, there are those who are consumed by the threats of transition. These managers are so paralyzed by prospects of change that they insist on clinging to the ways of the past, learn to recreate the past, or simply refuse to admit that the world they knew no longer exists (Easum, 1993). On the other hand, those open to the opportunities that always accompany transition understand that if people are allowed to become too comfortable with the present, they learn to live in the past (Easum, 1993).

In 1992, the theme of the 47th Annual Conference of the Association for Supervision and Curriculum Development (ASCD) was "Transforming Learning: Paradigms, Practices, and Possibilities." As one of the general session speakers for this conference, I spoke of the need for paradigm change that would allow educators to prepare students for success in a high-tech society. A paradigm is a set of assumptions, beliefs, ideas, values, or expectations that form a filter through which we make meaning out of life, create structure and process, view information, and make value judgments. According to Easum, our paradigms set boundaries in which we are willing to process information. Importantly, our paradigms also tell us how to solve problems (Easum, 1993). In 1992, ASCD recognized that our old paradigms had proven to be imperfect filters for the future vision we must have in order to meet the requirements of the 21st Century. By creating new paradigms, trying new practices, and imagining new possibilities, school leaders can transform learning for all students (Valient & Hill, 1992).

It is now more than a decade since ASCD alerted educators to the need for changing paradigms, but a shift in paradigms began long ago. North America has been caught between what "was" and has now disintegrated, and what is emerging or taking shape. This "crack in history" is expected to last until 2014 and will feature many shifts that will challenge leaders to devise new ways of solving old problems (Easum, 1993). The most important paradigm shifts for school officials and leaders are listed next.

The Age of Discovery is over, and the Age of Discernment has begun. Society is expected to experience a shift from innovation to application. Applying the newly discovered technologies will bring about new lifestyles, new ways of transmitting and assimilating knowledge, and new ways of performing tasks at home, in school, and in the workplace. In the emerging world, whoever controls information will control power.

Families will change in definition, constitution, and ethics. In 1990, the U.S. Census Bureau defined family as a group of two or more persons residing together and related by birth, marriage, or adoption. In the emerging world, family will be defined as a group of two or more people who intentionally live together for the purpose of loving and caring for each other regardless of gender or time commitment (Easum, 1993). Easum goes on to note that in the 21st Century:

- It will not be considered normal to live a lifetime with one spouse.

- Without a constant "center," most people will be broken, stressed out, and disjointed; sales of self-help books will soar.

- Over three quarters of the population will experience some form of abuse and over half of the population will be addicted to one drug or another (Gallop, 1989).

- AIDS will threaten the very foundation of society—especially among Blacks, Hispanics, and adolescents—and will continue to change patterns of behavior for decades.

Institutions will experience decline. People will trust individuals more than systems of thought or institutions and will bond with groups of people who provide relationships and meet their individual needs. Thus, small, secure groups will become the primary form of socializing (Easum, 1993).

Institutions that maintain their bureaucracies will vanish. Speed will rival the importance of quality in the emerging world as organizations streamline everything to respond more quickly to their customers. This will make "doing business" harder for bureaucracies, but easier for entrepreneurs. According to Easum, in the emerging world, leaders will be those willing to risk leaving the safety of the "good-ole-boy" system. Those tied to bureaucracies will vanish, while organizations that learn the most will produce the most (1993).

The middle class will continue to shrink in size. In the emerging world, there will be a steady decline in the average family's income with a steady increase in the ranks of the poor (Pear, 1991; Sine, 1991). Those businesses that focus on the needs of the middle class only will lose profits while those focusing on the needs of those at either the high or low end of the marketplace will thrive (Easum, 1993).

The role of cities will decline. Emphasis on neighborhoods will diminish as a regional mentality emerges. In the emerging world, many people will eat, play, socialize, and work in the same locale as more "edge cities" develop for those who can afford to live in them; cities will be dismantled altogether (Easum, 1993).

Use of print will change as sights and sounds dominate. As this century continues, the arts, typically enjoyed by the affluent and educated, and entertainment, normally enjoyed by the masses, will merge (Easum, 1993). Interactive television will become the way we perceive, assimilate, and interpret news and reality. The only print that survives this century will be electronic. Children will read books on computers and creatively change the stories as they read (Easum, 1993). According to Urice, during this century we will find that if something cannot be seen and experienced, it will not be heard or accepted (1989).

There will be a return to grass-roots participation. This return will then cause the restructuring of schools and every aspect of community life. Teamwork, diversity, and an emphasis on creativity will become the primary methods of profitability for all corporations (Shonk, 1992).

Importantly, the following are to be expected within a few decades:

- Giant monoliths will be replaced with webs of smaller enterprises that are encapsulated inside large businesses for accounting purposes (Mauer, 1992).

- Corporate executives (this includes school leaders) will have to be bilingual.

- Villages, towns, edge cities, provinces, counties, regions, and states will have more power than the federal government (Nisbitt, 1990).

Processing knowledge will be the primary skill of productive persons. People will have less use for memory or writing skills as knowledge will be processed purely from a global perspective; sequential, linear, rational, and deductive thinking will continue to disappear as collecting, storing, and retrieving knowledge becomes much less important than knowing how to process knowledge (O'Brien & Little, 1990).

Diversity will create new partnerships. Already more than 25% of the U.S. population is non-White. It has been projected that by the year 2010, a third of states in the United States will be "majority minority" (U.S. Census Bureau, 2000). Then, the culturally disadvantaged will be those young White people raised in the suburbs who are only able to converse in one language (Easum, 1993). Interracial marriages will continue to increase—producing many of the babies born in the 21st Century.

The "glass ceiling" will disappear. In the emerging society, the male-dominated world will be a thing of the past as the "glass ceiling," which prevented women from holding top-level jobs, will disappear. Inclusiveness will replace sexism in the job market (and in our schools as well) as male roles are redefined and reduced. As a new set of women's values infuse all areas of life, common employee benefits will come to include daycare, maternity/paternity leave, and the option of full- and part-time jobs at home (Radford-Ruether, 1983).

There will be a clash between hard work and easy living. In the 1980s, qualities such as obligation and duty were replaced with compassion and empathy as the Protestant work ethic was replaced with an emphasis on fulfillment and personal meaning. However, there is now a discernable clash between a need for quality products and a passion for more relaxed lifestyles. In the 21st Century, those who choose to play may not do as well financially as those who choose to work hard, but they will not regret the easier lifestyle (Easum, 1993).

Leading in an Ever-Changing Society

Given the present reality of our school situation and the constant cry of school communities for improved public schools, leaders and those officials in positions to facilitate change must engage in the practices most likely to produce positive results. An understanding of anticipated societal shifts (such as those previously discussed) should help today's school leaders in their preparation, planning, and ongoing effectiveness. According to Kiechel (1992), however, the most effective leaders are those who see themselves as "servant leaders." Servant leaders will be distinguished from other types of leaders because they:

- Are "stewards" who will take people and their work seriously

- Listen attentively and with compassion

- Take leads from grassroots movements

- Are self-effacing and not grandiose in style

Unless school officials and leaders develop leadership styles that can improve public education, home schooling and private school attendance will continue to grow. The continued clamor for vouchers by many organized Black and Hispanic parent groups will escalate if change in public education is not imminent.

Whether effective school leaders are at the building level, in the central office, the boardroom, or the classroom, they must constantly ask:

- "What are we doing that no longer works?"

- "Why are we still doing these things?"

- "What are the implications of not doing them?"

Most importantly, to be effective, leaders must enhance their own ability to use resources more creatively, be more innovative, and enhance their problem-solving abilities.

Using Resources More Creatively

Many school leaders know how to find the considerable amount of information that is available; however, leaders will stumble if they do not know how to use this information. Similarly, leaders who do not make the best of their human or fiscal resources will inevitably fail. Information or data should be gathered from outside of the school district rather than from within. For example, a school leader in a district where a company would be hiring many transient migrant and day workers realized the children of these workers would soon be enrolled in district schools. When he suggested to his employees that they develop an outreach plan to address the needs of children of migrant workers, many of his staff responded that there were no migrant children in the system. Clearly, this leader looked outside of his institution to find clues for future action.

Leaders must work to avoid the four deadly sins of inside-out thinking (Kami, 1988):

- **Complacency**—Believing that "if it ain't broke, don't fix it"

- **Blindness**—Being unable to see changes and paradigm shifts taking place all around

- **Megalomania**—Running a one-person show that relies on intuition

- **Pride**—Going for the short-term fix while ignoring the long-term solution

Being More Innovative

Good leaders are courageous enough to devise appropriate responses to their analysis of the information they have collected—even if it means destroying traditional practices. Drucker (1992) notes that a leader must have the moral character and willingness to make strategic decisions that allow the organization's mission to win over tradition. Tradition assumes that the experiences of one generation should be the norm for each succeeding generation—even though history shows that many traditions that brought new life to one generation do not always have the same effect for later generations.

School leaders who are creative and innovative in responding to the needs of their consumers may face resistance at first from traditional thinkers or those paralyzed by the prospects of change. However, leaders willing to involve their staffs in implementing practices for school improvement will be rewarded with improved staff morale and student achievement.

In his book, *Transitioning,* Dan Southerland (1999, pp. 8–19) provides a process for facilitating change for leaders who are convinced that change must occur. School leaders and visionaries may find these steps useful in their endeavors to prepare followers for change and the implementation of new ideas, goals, objectives, programs, and strategies:

1. Preparing for Vision
2. Defining the Vision
3. Planting the Vision
4. Sharing the Vision
5. Implementing the Vision
6. Dealing With the Opposition
7. Making Course Corrections
8. Evaluating the Results

Enhancing Problem-Solving Abilities

If no problems have been resolved and no change has occurred, there has been no leadership, only management. Problem solving usually involves good timing. When people are *proactive* rather than *reactive*, they can strategically plan actions. Problem solving usually involves:

- *Identifying the problem*—Is this the symptom of a bigger problem or the actual cause of the problem?

- *Brainstorming possible steps*—Every step must be carefully considered. Brainstorming the first five things to do, the next five things to do, and so on will help you avoid failure or setbacks. Explore the consequences of all possible options.

- *Taking action*—Implementing carefully developed action plans is the focal point of solving problems.

- *Following through*—This occurs after you have taken action. An analysis of what was done is necessary to identify improvements that can be made.

The goals and objectives developed by effective leaders will mirror the problems and issues they seek to address. Communication, of course, is critical to the success of any leader. Also critical is a clear understanding of the roles and responsibilities of all school leaders for those who want to enhance their own leadership effectiveness.

Roles and Responsibilities of School Leaders

During the mid-1970s, I worked for the National School Boards Association as director of urban and minority relations. In the early 1980s, I served as executive director of the National Alliance of Black School Educators. In both positions, I found conflicts between school boards and superintendents to be among the most debilitating for ongoing school success. While almost everyone knows that school boards govern and develop policy and that superintendents administer that policy, clarifying what these roles entail is not as simple as it sounds.

The Role of School Boards

In general, the role of the school board is to:

- Develop policy.

- Hire and evaluate the superintendent.

- Establish priorities as well as educational plans and programs.

- Approve and adopt an annual budget, in conjunction and collaboration with the superintendent.

- Establish salaries and salary schedules, terms and conditions of employment, fringe benefits, leave policies, and in-service training for all school employees.

Importantly, school boards are also responsible for the maintenance of school facilities and the development of public relations. They must avoid the temptation to dictate how the superintendent should manage day-to-day operations of the district. Such micromanagement is beyond the policy-making role of the school board (Reeves, 2003).

The Responsibilities of Superintendents

The superintendent's primary responsibility is to develop those administrative practices and procedures that will conform with school board policy. To do this effectively, superintendents must understand shifting paradigms, for they also serve as the chief advisor to the school board on educational matters. The superintendent must make certain the school board receives information necessary in order to make informed decisions (Reeves, 2003). As the advisor to the school board in setting priorities, the superintendent must not only articulate to the board the current and future needs of the district, but he or she should also suggest a process and develop appropriate strategies.

Whenever school boards and their superintendents have public battles, children are the ultimate losers. All too often, both sides claim it is the welfare of the children that has caused (and now justifies) their behavior or position. Yet personal agendas, oversized egos, and hidden motives often supercede genuine concern for children. To avoid public and divisive displays, school boards and superintendents must take precautionary measures before the employment contract is signed. Table 10.1 (page 231), "Do's and Don'ts of School Leadership," should help.

Community confidence increases when those who serve on the policy making (school board) side of a school district's leadership team join those who serve on the administrative side in showing the public that the school district is governed in a competent and collaborative fashion (Reeves, 2003). Moreover, school leaders can effectively address student educational needs and the desires of the school community when they understand how critical their cooperation and avoidance of conflict are to the ongoing process of school improvement. When they work together, they can facilitate the process for change and reclaim our youth.

The Role of Building Leaders

Those who lead at the building level as principals or assistant principals should also adhere to the do's and don'ts listed in Table 10.1 as they work with parent advisory teams, community school boards, and even student leadership organizations. Building principals and assistant principals have unique opportunities to create individual schools that are beacons of hope for the students and entire communities as well. The efficacy of using resources wisely and being more innovative and proactive in problem solving will benefit principals as much, if not more, than superintendents. However, principals are in a better position to excite teachers, counselors, parents, and other adults about the roles they can play as *Merchants of Hope.*

Table 10.1

Do's and Don'ts of School Leadership

Do	Don't
1. Have and show respect for individuals' diverse backgrounds.	1. Become biased or pejorative because of obvious or perceived differences among board and administrative team members.
2. Discuss and agree on roles and responsibilities of board members, their staffs, the superintendent, and administrative team members.	2. Dictate roles and responsibilities to administrative subordinates.
3. Have and show respect for the roles and responsibilities of others.	3. Allow self-importance, haughtiness, ego inflation, arrogance, or false pride to make you think you are more important than you really are.
4. Clarify, through discussions and writings, the respective expectations of both sides.	4. Assume everyone already knows what is expected.
5. Take time to share perceptions based on history, recent past, and previous developments, and to discuss implications for the future.	5. Ignore history or past developments and make plans without input from anyone who has a perspective on implications of previous developments for the future.
6. Help and heal.	6. Hurt and harm.
7. Build morale with positive praise and affirmation.	7. Belittle and demean through criticism and condescension.

Therefore, principals should make sure their discussion of roles and responsibilities also includes:

- A plan for developing a new teacher–veteran mentoring program in the school

- Plans for creating three-person teams of teachers with two very effective and positive members of the team paired with an ineffective teacher who can benefit from the advice and encouragement of the two positive veterans

- Regular review with school employees of the school's progress in meeting goals they have jointly set, discussed, and embraced

- Ongoing efforts to bring more resources to the school (for example, businesses to adopt the school and provide equipment, better-trained and committed teachers, and improved fiscal management)

- Improved communication both in school and to the school community, parents, and the superintendent (or superintendent designee)

- Ongoing efforts to lift spirits through praise and morale boosters

- A focus on time management (remember, children are in schools for approximately 6 hours each day; adults in those schools must make every minute count)

Because leadership is a process for promoting change, any school official, employee, student, or parent—regardless of position or title—can be a school leader. Change is constant, and our responses to changes around us must be as constant as well. It is my hope that this discussion of paradigm shifts and future trends expected in our emerging society over the next few decades will lead to careful collaboration in decision making. Preparing youth to live as leaders in a vastly different society will require much forethought, analysis, discussion, and deliberate effort, as well as the commitment and cooperation of all concerned *Merchants of Hope.* Therefore, school leaders must embrace and implement strategies for reform that will reclaim all youth, especially our Black and Hispanic students.

Recommendations for School Reform

This book is filled with strategies that can enhance the achievement of Black and Hispanic students. The most important priorities, however, are shared in the recommendations provided below:

- Issue a mission and policy statement for school districts and individual schools that indicates high expectations for all students.

- Establish an inviting school climate for Black and Hispanic students and their parents.

- Make certain every classroom is inviting and encouraging.

- Provide a multicultural curriculum.

- Promote an academically rich environment for all students.

- Establish goals to eliminate tracking and ability grouping.

- Establish goals to eliminate inter-district financial disparities and the "savage" intra-district inequalities that frustrate so many Black and Hispanic youth (Kozol, 1991).

- Introduce cooperative learning and heterogeneous grouping.

- Provide hands-on materials and opportunities for field experience.

- Promote the use of a variety of teaching styles.

- Encourage teachers to teach persistence.

- Use diagnostic evaluation.

- Develop plans to improve the effective level of parental involvement in your school district.

- Keep communities and businesses informed of good news and encourage successful businesses and churches to adopt schools and serve as mentors, tutors, and school partners.

Leading With Fortitude and Faith

As school leaders face what may appear to be an uncertain future, they can be inspired by the knowledge that they have both the fortitude and faith to foster change and reclaim youth. These youth, no matter how troubled they may seem, are indeed *our* future. Unless leaders focus on ways to facilitate change and necessary school improvement in these youth, the future will not be very promising.

The next chapter discusses how you can develop and maintain a focus on the future by first assessing where you are today.

Chapter 11

Focusing on the Future

Nothing in the world helps a man to keep healthy
so much as the knowledge of a life task.

—Anonymous

We owe it to ourselves and to our children to make certain the future reflects our best contributions. The time to plan for a secure, promising, and rewarding future is now. Educators have a golden opportunity to mold the future as few other Americans can. As astronaut Christa McAuliffe said, "I touch the future . . . I teach."

Our futures are jeopardized to the extent that we fail as a society to prepare Black and Hispanic students for purposeful and meaningful futures. Too many of these youth have no real concept of their futures, and live only for the day or moment. The suggestions in this book prove that we are not powerless, and that schools can affect the futures of these students. As educators, we can foster in them a real dream for a future and the ability to set goals for lifelong success. Schools can do what few other institutions can. They can tap into the greatness of each and every one of us.

This chapter gives you an opportunity to reflect on the main themes in this book and consider how they can improve your efforts to reach Black and Hispanic students.

One Final Attitude Check

Educators have the power to revitalize communities and put hope back into many lives. Thus, teaching should bring satisfaction; however, teachers are more likely to feel frustrated and dissatisfied when:

- They don't feel they are reaching certain children.

- They are not rewarded (professionally or personally) for the children they have reached and the achievement they have facilitated.

- They lose control of their classrooms.

- They are not respected by colleagues, supervisors, students, or parents.

- They do not receive support from within the school or school systems.

- Their efforts don't seem to make a difference in the quality of life for their students.

These feelings of frustration can be counteracted with strategies teachers can use to make a significant difference in the quality of life for their Black and Hispanic students. They can reach more students, derive more personal and professional gratification for a job well done, and maintain control of a respectful classroom. As a result, they will experience less frustration and more respect from colleagues, supervisors, and parents.

Instructional strategies that can make a difference are, however, often not easily implemented. Habitual attitudes and behaviors are not easily changed. Often, teachers find themselves halfheartedly implementing new strategies, but maintaining resistant attitudes. The next time you have a resistant attitude toward trying a new strategy, remember you are *too competent to lose confidence.* Have an open mind as you use the strategy, and give yourself time to determine whether it will work for you.

You have a golden opportunity to uplift countless students who *need* what you have to give. *You* need an attitude that knows no limitations to your power. Take time now to reassess how you really feel about the following:

1. Do you believe the problem is urgent? The underachievement of many Black and Hispanic students threatens the future of our communities, cities, counties, states, and indeed, our nation. Every concerned educator, parent, or citizen who can have a positive impact on the development of a young person must take advantage of opportunities to do so. Regardless of whether your school or community is 1% or 100% Black or Hispanic, immediate action must be taken.

2. How do you develop and communicate your expectations of Black and Hispanic students? Are you able to deal effectively with differences and diversity in students? To what extent do you allow differences in student race, class, physical appearance, speech, placement, behavior, or achievement to influence your opinions and expectations? Many adults and some teachers may innocently or inadvertently communicate negative feelings to students. All adults who interact with youth must determine whether they have engaged in verbal or nonverbal behavior that can send a negative message of low expectations to a particular student.

3. How highly do you value your role in augmenting the academic self-image of your Black and Hispanic students? Teachers and other school officials must appreciate not only the role they play in sharing knowledge and advice, but also see their interactions with all students as meaningful and motivational. As a professional, you must often take the first (and even second) step in saving the lives of students who are not meeting their full academic potential.

4. How much effort are you willing to make to help eradicate institutional racism in your school or school system? Educators must push for more pluralistic curricula and an elimination of tracking and ability grouping, as well as for more appropriate assessment instruments and procedures for Black and Hispanic students. Moreover, educators and concerned *Merchants of Hope* must eradicate the unfair practices and signs of individual and institutional bias that facilitate development of an oppositional identity and rejection of success in many Black and Hispanic youth.

5. How willing are you to change your style of teaching? If you understand that teaching and learning style differences can significantly undermine Black and Hispanic students' performance, you should seek to facilitate congruence between their learning styles and your teaching style.

6. Do you see something likable in all students? Unless school officials and other *Merchants of Hope* can lift up our children and give them genuine hope for a better future, children may be alienated and lose their motivation to live a meaningful life. Unless they feel a bond with adults and school personnel and develop confidence—through appreciation of their strengths—their fear of failure will keep many of them from ever realizing their self-worth and full potential. Moreover, many will develop a greater aversion for mainstream society and the principles needed for legitimate success and survival if they begin to think of school officials and other adults as the enemy.

7. Are you willing to set personal goals and help Black and Hispanic youth do the same? All *Merchants of Hope* should want professional gratification as well as the joy of building student bonds. It is important to set short- and long-term goals and priorities. Are teachers paid just to impart knowledge, or are they paid to develop thriving, successful human beings? Greater teaching satisfaction is derived by establishing professional goals and benchmarks for goal fulfillment. Whether you are a teacher, counselor, mentor, parent, or a *Merchant of Hope* who makes a living outside of traditional education, you should still set short- and long-range goals that will allow you to experience success at various stages of your relationship with youth.

8. Are you willing to establish the appropriate climate for student growth? This will require more creativity, better communication skills, enthusiasm, and an emphasis on building determination, diligence, and discipline. This also means adults will avoid behavior that debilitates, demeans, degrades, and destroys the students' desires to do well.

9. Are you willing to be more innovative in establishing good student discipline? Prevention strategies designed to enhance student motivation can improve student responsibility, self-control, and discipline. Yet their implementation requires commitment, persistence, and consistency.

10. How far are you willing to go to build effective partnerships with parents, home, and community? The achievement and discipline of Black and Hispanic students are improved when communities become a part of the education process (Duff & McClain, 1981). Teachers and schools can be the catalysts that foster the shared values and commitments of a community to its youth. No society can remain vital without a reasonable base of shared values; however, such values are not established by edict from lofty levels of the society. They are generated chiefly in the family, school, church, or other intimate settings in which people interact with one another face to face (Gardner, 1991). Schools (and their teachers and administrators) must be willing to do whatever it takes to gain necessary community and business support.

11. What are you willing to do to improve both equality and equity in education and access to opportunities for Black and Hispanic students? While we know that school desegregation and test bias have contributed to a lack of equity in our schools (Green & Griffore, 1978), this is no reason to run from opportunities to inspire diverse youth to overcome obstacles in their lives in their personal pursuit of excellence.

12. What are you willing to do to expand your knowledge of shifting paradigms so that plans are made to meet changing student needs? Those *Merchants of Hope* who are committed to reclaiming Black and Hispanic youth and others who may be at risk of school failure must remember the world these students will live in as adults. Many of the shifting paradigms mentioned in chapter 10 will take place during the adult lives of today's students. Today's adults must be mindful of these likely developments when teaching, counseling, and mentoring children and youth.

Marva Collins (Collins, Tamarkin, & Haley, 1990) once observed that you should teach as if your life depended on it. And in a real sense, it does. No one ever said teaching was easy. Your ability to put ideas into practice with a goal of preparing all students for meaningful futures can make teaching the most rewarding thing you could ever do.

By the same token, no one promises an easy path to anyone who reaches out to others. In fact, many self-help gurus discourage personal outreach, implying that it comes at the expense of personal development. I have found the opposite to be true. When we give of ourselves to help others, we discover so much more about ourselves. Enhanced personal development is one of the serendipities of personal service. Tavis Smiley (2002) notes that education must be the number one priority for every Black American. I submit that the education of Black and Hispanic youth must be the number one priority for anyone who cares about America. Caring *Merchants of Hope* must demand more from our schools, businesses, churches, and communities, and much more from ourselves as we unite to stand for children and to reclaim our hope for tomorrow.

Choosing to Make a Difference

I am convinced that anyone who endeavors to develop children is not only a magnificent *Merchant of Hope,* but also a true hero or heroine. Not only do I believe in teachers, I revere them. I also have the utmost admiration for those who take time to touch the lives of others. I know how overwhelming the challenge of developing individuals can appear to be at times. But the *real* challenge is the challenge of commitment. When more teachers increase their commitment and their repertoire of teaching techniques, more students will be able to succeed, and more educators will reap the *real* joy this profession is capable of providing. When adults enhance their compassion so they can counsel and mentor needy youth, more lives will be enriched, fewer children will be left behind, and our nation will reap the joy of better tomorrows and a more fascinating future.

Rather than ignore the problem or run from the challenge, rather than lament all of the telltale signs of human, moral, and social decay in our communities, each of us can facilitate long-term solutions to our problems. The problems caused by the underachievement of so many Black and Hispanic youth will continue to escalate unless there is a total school effort to solve problems and enhance the collective commitment of caring communities. If I didn't believe in the gratifying greatness and ability of educators and other *Merchants of Hope,* I would not have written this book. My prayer is that every reader is inspired to dig just a little deeper and become even more committed to helping our children and youth. You deserve the good feelings that professional excellence and student success are sure to bring. Not only must you believe you can make a difference— you must also *choose* to make a difference. Good luck!

Focusing Your Efforts

He who knows the why of living surmounts every how . . .

—Nietzsche

I hope this book has enhanced your understanding of why you are so important in facilitating the success of Black and Hispanic students. How you fulfill your professional responsibilities from this day forward will say much about you, both as a person and as a professional. The following worksheets will assist you in your endeavors to bring out the best in Black and Hispanic children.

Worksheet A, "Indicators of Poor Student Self-Image" (page 247), can help you determine whether a student has a low academic self-image, a low social self-image, or both.

Worksheet B, "Teaching Behaviors That Improve Student Achievement" (page 250) can serve as a self-evaluation, and provides the opportunity for teachers to improve their approach to increasing student achievement and development. With this worksheet, teachers, school leaders, and other *Merchants of Hope* can enhance ongoing efforts to improve the multicultural environment of the school, enhance their teaching styles, improve their students' higher order thinking skills, and enhance their efforts to implement heterogeneous grouping, cooperative learning, and peer tutoring/coaching strategies. Importantly, these worksheets will help school officials monitor progress in teaching students higher order thinking skills and abating the effects of the fear of failure and student rejection of success, thus improving student discipline, school and classroom climate, and the home/school bond.

Worksheet C, "Student Activities That Enhance Self-Image" (page 260), includes activities to help students improve their self-image and their academic achievement.

Worksheet D, "Counseling and Mentoring Behaviors That Improve Student Motivation" (page 261), provides opportunities for self-evaluation so that those parents, counselors, mentors, and *Merchants of Hope* who are not teachers but nonetheless choose to make a difference in the lives of youth will have benchmarks that can ultimately enhance their effectiveness in facilitating positive youth development.

Worksheet E, "Leadership Skills for Facilitating Student Success and School Improvement" (page 263), includes a checklist to help school board members, superintendents, and building administrators improve their effectiveness as agents of change.

WORKSHEET A
Indicators of Poor Student Self-Image

The following are a number of characteristics of a poor self-image in children and youth. They are grouped into academic and social behaviors. Use this list to assess an individual child's academic and social self-images.

This assessment tool will help you determine what strategies to use when assisting students. The extent to which children show any of these behaviors will dictate the urgency and intensity of your response. For example, the signs of a poor academic self-image require immediate assistance. The student who frequently expresses dislike for school, the teacher, or both will require one-on-one dialogue, parental support, and intervention with the strategies discussed in chapter 5. Likewise, students who show signs of a poor social self-image will benefit from the strategies discussed in chapters 5 through 8 of this book.

Check the appropriate column on the right.
F = Frequently   S = Sometimes   R = Rarely

POOR ACADEMIC SELF-IMAGE To what extent does the student . . .	F	S	R
1. Fail to complete work?			
2. Show hostile behavior?			
3. Use defiant speech?			
4. Daydream?			
5. Show little or no eye contact?			
6. Make excuses?			
7. Give up too easily?			
8. Skip school or arrive tardy?			

REPRODUCIBLE

WORKSHEET A (continued)

POOR ACADEMIC SELF-IMAGE To what extent does the student . . .	F	S	R
9. Fail to volunteer or participate?			
10. Withdraw and isolate himself or herself?			
11. Express dislike for school, the teacher, or both?			
12. Exhibit facial expressions and body movements that show frustration, anxiety, or pain?			

POOR SOCIAL SELF-IMAGE To what extent does the student . . .	F	S	R
1. Lack confidence in performing before others?			
2. Fail to demonstrate ability in such social skills as sports, dancing, "playing the dozens," or rapping?			
3. Function in a support group of peers?			
4. Exhibit interest in social activities such as dancing, listening to music, or sports activities?			
5. Show little or no eye contact?			
6. Persist in learning social skills (card playing, music, or sports)?			
7. Demonstrate friendly, sincere behavior?			
8. Dress in a slovenly manner and show poor personal hygiene?			
9. Have poor eating habits?			

WORKSHEET A (continued)			
POOR SOCIAL SELF-IMAGE **To what extent does the student . . .**	**F**	**S**	**R**
10. Try too hard to please?			
11. Cry easily?			
12. Use facial expressions and body language that show pain, anxiety, or frustration?			

Adapted from Kuykendall, C. (1989). *Improving Black Student Achievement Through Enhancing Self-Image.* Washington, DC: Mid-Atlantic Equity Center.

WORKSHEET B
Teaching Behaviors That Improve Student Achievement

This is a self-checklist that you can use to determine your strengths in improving achievement motivation in youth, and areas in which you may want to expand your knowledge and skills. There are two categories:

☑ Check "+" if you are comfortable with your knowledge and skills in this area and exhibit appropriate and consistent behavior.

☑ Check "−" if you need to strengthen your knowledge and skills and demonstrate appropriate behaviors consistently.

If you have minus signs on your completed assessment, you should consider developing a personal action plan with a timetable to implement strategies and activities that will increase your effectiveness in reaching and teaching all students. Your personal action plan should focus on steps you will take in the appropriate categories. You might also choose to pursue additional learning for yourself or your staff in these areas through workshops or staff development exercises.

CREATING A MULTICULTURAL ENVIRONMENT As a teacher, how do you rate yourself on . . .	+	−
1. Reviewing reading materials and school tests to identify culturally sensitive materials and take steps to minimize their impact on students?		
2. Identifying and notifying school officials of any policies or procedures that inadvertently penalize certain races, cultures, sexes, or disabilities?		
3. Understanding and teaching African-American and Hispanic-American history and culture?		

WORKSHEET B (continued)

CREATING A MULTICULTURAL ENVIRONMENT As a teacher, how do you rate yourself on . . .	+	−
4. Developing classroom activities that foster an understanding and appreciation of the struggle of Black Americans against slavery?		
5. Providing opportunities for students of different racial and ethnic groups to interact?		
6. Identifying and discussing in class recent and contemporary examples of overt racism (such as racism under Apartheid in South Africa)?		
7. Integrating appreciation for cultural diversity into all of your classroom activities?		
8. Recognizing and pointing out to students values that strengthen cultural bonds?		
9. Constructing and using heterogeneous groups?		
10. Distinguishing between equality and equity and knowing when to treat students the same or differently on the basis of their race, ethnic group, disability, culture, sex, or level of academic achievement?		
11. Allowing students to engage in activities that will enhance their appreciation of the cultural strengths of all diverse groups?		
USING A VARIETY OF TEACHING STYLES **As a teacher, how do you rate yourself on . . .**	**+**	**−**
1. Encouraging personal interaction, including hugs, touching, and affectionate pats?		
2. Identifying students' strengths and weaknesses in how they learn?		

WORKSHEET B (continued)

USING A VARIETY OF TEACHING STYLES As a teacher, how do you rate yourself on . . .	+	−
3. Using instructional strategies that allow students to build on their strengths and overcome their weaknesses?		
4. Explaining how class content is related to the students' experiences?		
5. Encouraging more student grouping and interaction that leads to greater student achievement and appreciation of diversity?		
6. Developing rapport with each of your students?		
7. Conducting classroom activities that allow for the emotional and physical involvement of Black and Hispanic youth?		
8. Using positive slogans and inspirational messages all over the classroom?		
9. Using the buddy system?		
10. Using eye contact in a supportive way?		
11. Using alternative instructional strategies, such as cooperative learning and peer coaching?		
USING COOPERATIVE AND FLEXIBLE GROUPING As a teacher, how do you rate yourself on . . .	+	−
1. Using heterogeneous grouping rather than ability grouping and tracking?		
2. Using more diagnostic pre-testing to enhance the heterogeneous grouping process?		

WORKSHEET B (continued)

USING COOPERATIVE AND FLEXIBLE GROUPING As a teacher, how do you rate yourself on . . .	+	−
3. Providing more opportunities for teacher-student interaction?		
4. Employing some forms of cooperative learning groups?		
5. Setting up and using a peer tutoring or coaching system?		
6. Using a greater variety of learning materials and activities?		
7. Providing more frequent use of high-quality feedback?		
8. Re-grouping students at regular intervals?		
TEACHING HIGHER ORDER THINKING SKILLS As a teacher, how do you rate yourself on . . .	+	−
1. Using open-ended and essay questions that foster active involvement and reflections?		
2. Providing opportunities for critical thinking through open-ended questions?		
3. Providing opportunities for divergent thinking by asking students to compare and contrast?		
4. Providing opportunities for inductive thinking by asking students to reason from the specific to the general?		
5. Providing opportunities for deductive thinking by specifically asking students to reason from the general to the specific?		

WORKSHEET B (continued)

TEACHING HIGHER ORDER THINKING SKILLS As a teacher, how do you rate yourself on . . .	+	−
6. Using one-to-one cajoling, probing, delving, and inspiring to help children develop their thinking powers?		
7. Allowing students to differentiate, integrate, and reintegrate to develop competence in representational thinking?		
8. Providing opportunities for higher-level distancing and metacognitive activities?		
9. Providing opportunities for more role plays, simulation planning, and evaluations?		
10. Providing regular opportunities for problem solving?		

OVERCOMING FEAR OF FAILURE AND REJECTION OF SUCCESS As a teacher, how do you rate yourself on . . .	+	−
1. Identifying students' unique talents and nonacademic strengths and building on those to foster confidence and overcome academic weaknesses?		
2. Using peers positively to identify strengths and encourage success through group activities?		
3. Using the buddy system?		
4. Developing a positive and cooperative relationship with the parent or guardian?		
5. Celebrating individual student accomplishments throughout the school year?		

WORKSHEET B (continued)

OVERCOMING FEAR OF FAILURE AND REJECTION OF SUCCESS As a teacher, how do you rate yourself on . . .	+	−
6. Helping students set short- and long-range goals?		
7. Allowing for weekly reviews of famous Black and Hispanic Americans who have set goals and achieved them?		
8. Setting monthly academic achievement goals for each child that can be shared with parents or guardians?		
9. Using the Success Chart (page 120)?		
10. Using activities to improve student motivation to succeed?		
11. Helping students with learning disabilities become more successful?		

IMPROVING OVERALL COMMITMENT As a teacher, how do you rate yourself on . . .	+	−
1. Projecting an image that tells students you are here to build rather than destroy them as people?		
2. Letting students know that you are aware of and interested in them as individuals?		
3. Conveying your experiences and confidence that each student can meet well-defined standards of values and demands for competence and can follow guidance toward solutions or problems?		
4. Enhancing the academic expectations and evaluations that parents or guardians hold for their children's ability?		

WORKSHEET B (continued)

IMPROVING OVERALL COMMITMENT As a teacher, how do you rate yourself on . . .	+	−
5. Serving as a model of sensitivity and high ideals for each student?		
6. Taking every opportunity to establish effective private (one-on-one) or semi-private communications with students?		
7. Encouraging students to express their opinions and ideas?		
8. Conveying to students concern and interest for their needs?		
9. Making certain the classroom climate is inviting physically and emotionally?		
10. Exhibiting enthusiasm for learning tasks and for the students?		
11. Interjecting humor into the classroom?		
12. Making a concerted effort to interact with each student?		
13. Encouraging students to praise their peers?		
14. Setting realistic but challenging expectations for students?		
15. Showing a desire to learn more about the various cultures represented in your classroom?		
16. Providing opportunities for all students to shine?		
17. Working with each student to establish goals, develop strengths, and overcome weaknesses?		

WORKSHEET B (continued)		
PROMOTING IMPROVED STUDENT DISCIPLINE **As a teacher, how do you rate yourself on . . .**	**+**	**–**
1. Having a positive attitude and a genuine "like" for all students?		
2. Building on the nonacademic strengths of all students?		
3. Providing students with tasks to improve their sense of responsibility?		
4. Showing respect, trust, a caring attitude, and a loving touch?		
5. Punishing student behavior rather than students?		
6. Using disciplinary actions to instruct rather than to punish?		
7. Rewarding and complimenting students for good behavior?		
8. Developing creative and effective alternatives to suspension?		
IMPROVING SCHOOL AND CLASSROOM CLIMATE **As a teacher, how do you rate yourself on . . .**	**+**	**–**
1. Using bright, warm, and decorative classroom colors?		
2. Highlighting accomplishments of local heroes and heroines?		
3. Displaying individual work and accomplishments of all students?		
4. Fostering mutual trust and respect between students?		

WORKSHEET B (continued)

IMPROVING SCHOOL AND CLASSROOM CLIMATE As a teacher, how do you rate yourself on . . .	+	−
5. Fostering mutual helpfulness between students?		
6. Moving around the class so that all students feel greater physical proximity with you?		
7. Monitoring student progress?		
8. Fostering freedom of student expression?		
9. Showing empathic understanding?		
10. Showing an interest in the child as a person?		

How do you rate yourself on . . .	+	−
1. Developing in all school personnel a positive commitment to student achievement?		
2. Setting appropriate standards for student behavior?		
3. Maintaining a purposeful, safe, and orderly environment?		

STRENGTHENING THE HOME/SCHOOL BOND As a teacher, how do you rate yourself on . . .	+	−
1. Understanding that parental involvement should encompass more than at-home responsibilities?		
2. Relating to parents with an attitude that conveys respect?		
3. Making positive telephone calls with good news on student behavior?		
4. Helping parents to understand that your role is to help the child grow in many ways?		

WORKSHEET B (continued)		
STRENGTHENING THE HOME/SCHOOL BOND **As a teacher, how do you rate yourself on . . .**	**+**	**−**
5. Educating more parents about the school's expectations of them?		
6. Sharing information with parents that will build understanding, knowledge, and trust?		
7. Encouraging parents to become a part of established parent organizations?		
8. Pushing for annual "Family Nights" in your school?		
9. Finding and using other resources in the community?		
10. Making use of community role models and mentors?		
11. Creating partnerships with community businesses and other youth-serving organizations, agencies, or institutions?		

Adapted from Kuykendall, C. (1989). *Improving Black Student Achievement Through Enhancing Self-Image.* Washington, DC: Mid-Atlantic Equity Center.

WORKSHEET C
Student Activities That Enhance Self-Image

Following is a list of activities for students that enhance their self-images. If you regularly provide a particular activity in your classroom, check the blank to the left of that activity. If you don't provide opportunities for this activity, check the blank on the right. You may want to expand your repertoire if you have more checks on the right than you have on the left.

Provide   **Don't Provide**

❏   1. Activities in which students can entertain classmates   ❏
        and/or display nonacademic talents and strengths
        as well as academic gifts

❏   2. Activities in which students can engage in such social   ❏
        skills as dancing, sports events, rapping, singing, or
        dramatic readings

❏   3. Peer tutoring and group projects where students can   ❏
        develop mutually supportive systems with peers

❏   4. Practical skills that allow students to repeat in rhyme   ❏

❏   5. Nonstructured and challenging games, puzzles, and   ❏
        activities with no deadline for completion

❏   6. Activities designed to help students be successful   ❏
        by working on challenging yet achievable goals

❏   7. Activities involving the use of pantomime   ❏

❏   8. Multicultural subject content and activities   ❏

❏   9. Activities that foster concentration and require long   ❏
        attention spans

❏ 10. Learning centers relating to subject matter and   ❏
        student interests

❏ 11. Activities that explore different types of families   ❏
        and the cultural strengths of each

❏ 12. Activities that highlight the unique strengths and   ❏
        special talents of each student

WORKSHEET D
Counseling and Mentoring Behaviors That Improve Student Motivation

This checklist gives *Merchants of Hope* who are in non-teaching positions the ability to improve their effectiveness in motivating youth. Understanding your strengths and weaknesses allows you to focus on helping students in ways that best suit you and to improve in those areas where you may not have as much experience or expertise.

Check "+" if you are comfortable with your ability in this area. Check "−" if you know you need improvement in this area.

UNDERSTANDING THE POWER YOU HAVE TO FOSTER YOUTH DEVELOPMENT As a *Merchant of Hope*, how do you rate yourself on . . .	+	−
1. Understanding *why* you need to become more involved in improving the achievement and behavior of youth who are not your own		
2. Your training and preparation to be an effective counselor, mentor, or *Merchant of Hope*		
3. Your ability to give unbiased advice		
4. Your ability to build on student strengths		
5. Your ability to help youth avoid negative peer pressure		
6. Your ability to help youth develop confidence in their abilities		
7. Your ability to listen		
8. Your ability to help youth understand how to resolve conflicts with parents and authority figures		

WORKSHEET D (continued)

UNDERSTANDING THE POWER YOU HAVE TO FOSTER YOUTH DEVELOPMENT As a *Merchant of Hope,* how do you rate yourself on . . .	+	–
9. Your convictions about encouraging self-love, pride, and abstinence in sexual relations		
10. Your ability to help youth say "no" to drugs		
11. Your ability to help youth set short- and long-term goals, which may include college		
12. Your ability to help youth who have been incarcerated avoid recidivism		
13. Your willingness to help youth "job shadow" for at least one day out of the year		
14. Your ability to enhance anger management and mediation skills in youth		
15. Your readiness to serve as a mentor to youth and their peers		

UNDERSTANDING HOW TO MAGNIFY YOUR POWER AS A *MERCHANT OF HOPE* How do you rate yourself on . . .	+	–
1. Your willingness to improve your skills in motivating and inspiring youth		
2. Understanding your own time limitations.		
3. Utilizing your own nonacademic strengths to enhance your efforts		
4. Avoiding stressful situations.		
5. Growing through the advice and counsel of persons who can mentor you		
6. Persisting when students are resisting		

WORKSHEET E
Leadership Skills for Facilitating
Student Success and School Improvement

Whether your job is a "leadership" position or not, you can use this checklist to determine your effectiveness in facilitating requisite change in your school or district.

Check "+" if you feel you've made substantial progress in this area. Check "−" if you know you need to improve your efforts.

As a leader, how do you rate yourself on . . .	+	−
1. Facilitating change and helping others to embrace change and consider its inevitability		
2. Understanding how future trends and paradigm shifts will impact important school decisions, such as what should be taught and how		
3. Using human and fiscal resources wisely		
4. Implementing alternatives to school suspension		
5. Enhancing the level of parental involvement in your classroom, school, district, or community		
6. Communicating with students and other school employees		
7. Fulfilling the responsibilities of your particular job		
8. Clarifying roles and responsibilities when confusion seems to reign		
9. Bringing order to disorderly and chaotic situations		
10. Uplifting employees and improving morale		
11. Improving the attitudes and behaviors of ineffective and negative teachers		

WORKSHEET E (continued)		
As a leader, how do you rate yourself on . . .	**+**	**−**
12. Providing regular reviews and evaluations of employee performance		
13. Increasing the hiring and retention of Black and Hispanic teachers and administrators		
14. Improving the school and classroom climate		
15. Serving as a mentor to a new employer or student		
16. Pairing positive veteran teachers with new teachers who they can mentor		

References

Akbar, N. (1991). *Visions for Black men*. Nashville, TN: Winston-Derek Publishers.

American Association of Colleges for Teacher Education. (1973). *No one model American*. Washington, DC: Author.

American Association of Colleges for Teacher Education. (1999). *National project to improve teacher education*. Washington, DC: Author.

American Council on Education. (2003). *Minorities in higher education: 20th annual status report*. Washington, DC: Author.

Armour, S. (2002, January 14). Minority job losses shrink gains made in the 90s. *USA Today*, B1.

Asante, K. M. (1994). *Classical Africa*. Maywood, NJ: The Peoples Publishing Group.

Bailey, D. (2001). School choice: The option of success. In J. Dewart (Ed.), *The state of Black America* (pp. 101–114). New York: The National Urban League.

Banks, J., & Grombs, J. (Eds.). (1972). *Black self concept*. New York: McGraw-Hill.

Beane, D. (1988). *Mathematics and science: Critical filters for the futures of minority students*. Washington, DC: Mid-Atlantic Equity Center.

Bell, Jr., C. (1985). *Explaining the progressively decreasing scores on Comprehensive Tests of Basic Skills (CTBS) of the school children of the District of Columbia public schools as they progress from elementary school into high school*. (ERIC Document Reproduction Service No. ED226234).

Berube, M. (1984). *Education and poverty: Effective schooling in the United States and Cuba*. Westport, CT: Greenwood Publishing.

Bonsteel, A. (2001, February 1). One in four U.S. students drops out. *School Reform News*. Available at www.heartland.org/PublicationIssue.cfm?pblId=6&pisId=97 (retrieved August 27, 2003).

Bradock, J. H., II, Dawkins, M. P., & Wilson, G. (1995). Intercultural contact and race relations among American youth. In W. D. Hawley & A. W. Jackson (Eds.), *Toward a common destiny: Improving race and ethnic relations in America* (pp. 237–256). San Francisco: Jossey-Bass.

Brophy, J. E., & Good, T. L. (1974). *Teacher-student relationships: Causes and consequences.* New York: Holt, Rinehart and Winston.

Burnette, J. (1999). *Critical behaviors and strategies for teaching culturally diverse students* (Report No. EDO-EC-99-12). Washington, DC: Special Education Programs. (ERIC Document Reproduction Service No. ED435147).

Carbo, M. (1996, July). *Improving reading test scores.* Paper presented at the National Reading Styles Conference, San Antonio, TX.

Carbo, M. (1997). *What every principal should know about teaching reading.* Syosset, NY: National Reading Styles Institute.

Cardenas, B., & Chahin, J. (2000). *Qualitative utilization: Focused evaluation of six high functioning HOSTS sites.* Dallas, TX: HOSTS Corporation.

Carnegie Council on Adolescent Development, Task Force on Education of Young Adolescents. (1989). *Turning points: Preparing American youth for the 21st century: The report of the Task Force on Education of Young Adolescents.* Washington, DC: Author.

Cheyney, L., Fine, M., & Ravitch, D. (1987). *American memory: A report on the humanities in the nation's public schools.* Washington, DC: National Endowment for the Humanities.

Children's Defense Fund. (1985). *Black and White children in America: Key facts.* Washington, DC: Author.

Choy, S. J., & Dodd, D. H. (1976, April). Standard-English-speaking and non-standard Hawaiian on English-speaking children: Comprehension of both dialects and teachers' evaluations. *Journal of Educational Psychology, 68*(2), 184–193. (ERIC Document Reproduction Service No. EJ142029).

Clifford, M. M., & Walster, E. (1973, Spring). Research note: The effect of physical attractiveness on teacher expectations. *Sociology of Education, 46,* 248.

Clinton, H. (1996). *It takes a village: And other lessons children teach us.* New York: Simon & Schuster.

Collins, M., Tamarkin, C., & Haley, A. (1990). *Marva Collins' way.* Los Angeles: J.P. Tarcher.

Cook, S. (1998). *Too blessed to be stressed: Words of wisdom for women on the move.* Nashville, TN: Thomas Nelson.

Cooper, H. M. et al. (1979, September). *Understanding Pygmalion: The social psychology of self-fulfilling classroom expectations.* Paper presented at the 87th Annual Convention of the American Psychological Association (New York). (ERIC Document Reproduction Service No. ED182642).

Cooper, H. M., Baron, R. M., & Louie, C. A. (1975, April). The importance of race and social class information in the formation of expectancies about academic performance. *Journal of Educational Psychology, 67,* 213–319. (ERIC Document Reproduction Service No. EJ120185).

Council on Interracial Books for Children. (1984). Fact sheet on institutional racism. New York: Author.

Daubenmier, J. (1990, March 11). Children learn lessons by staying away from school education. *Los Angeles Times, 27.*

Denbo, S. (1986). *Improving multicultural student achievement: Focus on the classroom.* Washington, DC: Mid-Atlantic Equity Center.

Denbo, S. (1987). *Improving minority achievement: Focus on the classroom.* Washington, DC: Mid-Atlantic Equity Center.

Dickerman, M. (1996). Teaching cultural pluralism. In J. Banks (Ed.), *Teaching strategies for ethnic studies.* Boston: Allyn & Bacon.

Donald, D. H. (1995). *Lincoln.* New York: Simon & Shuster.

Drucker, P. (1992). *Managing the future: The 1990s and beyond.* New York: Penguin Books.

DuBois, W.E.B. (1907). *The Negro and socialism.* New York: Horizon.

DuBois, W.E.B. (1968). *The autobiography of W.E.B. DuBois: A soliloquy of my life from the last decade of its first century.* New York: International Publishers.

Duff, O. B., & McClain, H. J. (Eds.). (1981). *Student concerns: Discipline, academic achievement and community involvement in a desegregated setting proceedings (December 13–14, 1979).* (ERIC Document Reproduction Service No. ED210362).

Dunkin, M. J., & Biddle, B. J. (1974). *The study of teaching.* New York: Holt, Rinehart & Winston.

Easum, W. (1993). *Dancing with dinosaurs.* Nashville, TN: Abingdon Press.

Edelman, M. (2001, March 16). Reminder: Adults shape children. *USA Today,* B1.

Edmonds, R. P. (1980). Effective education for minority pupils: Brown confounded or confirmed. In D. Bell (Ed.), *Shades of Brown: New perspectives of school desegregation.* New York: Teachers College Press.

Fagan, J., & Jones, S. J. (1984). Toward a theoretical model for intervention with violent juvenile offenders. In R. Mathias (Ed.), *Violent youth offenders.* San Francisco: National Council on Crime and Delinquency.

Fair, G. W. (1980, May). Coping with double-barreled discrimination. *Journal of School Health, 50,* 275–276.

Fine, M. (1986, Spring). Why urban adolescents drop into and out of public high schools. *Teachers College Record, 87,* 393–408.

Fletcher, M. (2001, April 7). Tests show wider gap in reading skills. *The Washington Post,* p. A02.

Fletcher, M. (2002, March 18). Diversity index used to achieve desegregation in San Francisco schools. *The Washington Post,* p. A01.

Fordham, S., & Ogbu, J. (1986). Black students' school success: Coping with the burden of acting White. *The Urban Review, 18*(3), 176–206.

Fulghum, R. (1993). *All I really need to know I learned in kindergarten: Uncommon thoughts on common things.* New York: Ballantine.

Gaden, T. (1992, May/June). Technology and the future of business. *The Futurist, 26.*

Gallop, G., Jr. (1989, November 17). Tracking America's soul. *Christianity Today.*

Gardner, J. W. (1991, September). *Building communities.* Paper presented at the Leadership Studies Program of the Independent Sector of Washington, DC.

Gay, G. (1990). Achieving educational equality through curriculum desegregation. *Phi Delta Kappan, 72*(1), 56–62.

Gilbert, S., & Gay, G. (1985, October). Improving the success in school of poor Black children. *Phi Delta Kappan, 67*(2), 133–137.

Gilmore, J., & Gilmore, E. (1982). *Give your child a future.* Englewood Cliffs, NJ: Prentice Hall.

Ginott, H. (1969). *Between parent and child: New solutions to old problems.* London: Staples Press.

Gipps, C. V. (1996). *A fair test? Assessment, achievement & equity.* Philadelphia: Open Press University.

Glasgow, D. (1980). *The Black underclass: Poverty, unemployment and entrapment of ghetto youth.* San Francisco: Jossey-Bass.

Gollub, W. L., & Sloan, E. (1978, April). Teacher expectations and race and socioeconomic status. *Urban Education, 13,* 95–106. (ERIC Document Reproduction Service No. EJ180582).

Good, T. L. (1981, February). Teacher expectations and student perceptions: A decade of research. *Educational Leadership, 38*(5), 415–422.

Good, T. L., & Brophy, J. E. (1973). *Looking in classrooms.* New York: Harper & Row.

Graves, E. G. (1978, September). Public education: Blame for many. *Black Enterprise, 9,* 7.

Green, R. L., & Griffore, R. J. (1978, Fall). School desegregation, testing and the urgent need for equity. *Education, 99,* 16–19.

Hale-Benson, J. (1982). *Black children: Their roots, culture and learning styles.* Provo, UT: Brigham Young University Press.

Hale-Benson, J. (1986). *Black children: Their roots, culture, and learning styles* (Rev. ed.). Baltimore: Johns Hopkins University Press.

Hammond, L. (1985). *Equality and excellence: Educational status of Black Americans.* New York: The College Board.

Hare, B. R. (1979). *Black girls: A comparative analysis of self-perceptions and achievement by race, sex and socioeconomic background.* Baltimore, MD: Johns Hopkins University Center for Social Organization of Schools.

Hare, B. R. (2001). *Black youth at-risk.* Unpublished manuscript.

Harnischfeger, A., & Wiley, D. E. (1980, September). *High school learning, vocational tracking, and what then? Contractor report.* Washington, DC: Statement to the Subcommittee on Elementary, Secondary and Vocational Education. (ERIC Document Reproduction Service No. ED212847).

Harrison, L. E., & Huntington, P. (Eds.). (2000). *Culture matters: How values shape human progress.* New York: Basic Books.

Harry, B., & Anderson, M. G. (1994). *The disproportionate representation of minority students in special education: Theories and recommendations.* Alexandria, VA: National Association of State Directors of Special Education.

Hawkins v. Coleman, 475 F. 2d 1278 (1973).

Haycock, K. (2001). Helping all students achieve! CLOSING the achievement gap. *Educational Leadership, 58,* 6.

Haycock, K., & Weiner, R. (2003, April). *Adequate yearly progress under the NCLB.* Paper presented at the National Center on Education and the Economy Policy Forum, Implementing the No Child Left BehindAct, in Washington, DC.

Heller, K. A., Holtzman, W. H., & Messick, S. (Eds.). (1982). *Placing children in special education: A strategy for equity.* Washington, DC: National Academy Press.

Henderson, A. (1987). *The evidence continues to grow: Parent involvement improves student achievement.* Columbia, MD: National Committee for Citizens in Education.

Henderson, A. T., & Map, K. L. (2002). *A new wave of evidence: The impact of school, family and community connections on student achievement.* Austin, TX: National Center for Family and Community Connections with Schools, Southwest Educational Development Laboratory.

Henderson, A., Marburger, C., & Oams, T. (1989). *Beyond the bake sale: An educator's guide to working with parents.* Columbia, MD: National Committee for Citizens in Education.

Herrnstein, R. J., & Murray, C. (1996). *The bell curve: Intelligence and class structure in American life.* New York: Simon & Schuster.

Hilliard, III., A. G. (1976). *Alternatives to I.Q. testing: An approach to the identification of gifted "minority" children* (Final Report to the California Department of Education). Sacramento, CA: California Department of Education. (ERIC Document Reproduction Service No. ED147009).

Hobson v. Hansen, 269 F. Supp 401 (1967).

Holloman, J. H. (2002). Redesigning professional development: Mentoring for diversity. *Educational Leadership, 59*(6): 88–89.

Howard, B. (1987). *Learning to persist, persisting to learn.* Washington, DC: Mid-Atlantic Equity Center.

Howard, J. (1985, December 12). Race and how it affects our everyday life. *Detroit Free Press,* p. A10.

Iyewarun, S. (1997, April). *A new look at Afrocentric curriculum.* Paper presented at the Rocky Mountain/Great Plains Regional Social Studies Conference, Overland Park, KS.

Jaap, J. (1999). Addressing diversity: Growing our own teachers in an urban setting. *The Forum, 7*(2), 3–4.

Jackson, A., & Davis, G. (2000). *Turning points: Educating adolescents in the 21st century.* New York: Teachers College Press.

Jones, K. M. (1986, March). The Black male in jeopardy. *The Crisis, 93,* 16–21, 41–42.

Kami, M. (1988). *Trigger points: The nine critical factors for growth and profit.* New York: McGraw-Hill.

Kaufman, P., Kwon, J. Y., Klein, S., & Chapman, C. D. (2000, November). *Dropout rates in the United States: 1999.* Washington, DC: National Center for Education Statistics, Institute of Education Sciences, U.S. Department of Education.

Kiechel, III, W. (1992, May 4). The leader as servant. *Fortune, 125,* 121–122.

Kimbro, D., & Hill, N. (1992). *Think and grow rich: A Black choice.* New York: Fawcett Books.

Knowles, L., & Prewitt, K. (1969). *Institutional racism in America.* Englewood Cliffs, NJ: Prentice Hall.

Kozol, J. (1991). *Savage inequalities: Children in America's schools.* New York: Crown Publishers.

Kunjufu, J. (1985). *Countering the conspiracy to destroy Black boys.* Chicago: African-American Images.

Kuykendall, C. (1975). *Developing leadership for parent/citizen groups.* Columbia, MD: National Committee for Citizens in Education.

Kuykendall, C. (1977). *Citizens' Training Institute report on effectiveness of parent training.* Columbia, MD: National Committee for Citizens in Education.

Kuykendall, C. (1986). *Counselor attitudes toward delinquent youth.* Unpublished manuscript.

Kuykendall, C. (1987). *You and yours: Making the most of this school year.* Washington, DC: Mid-Atlantic Equity Center.

Kuykendall, C. (1989). *Improving Black student achievement through enhancing self-image.* Washington, DC: Mid-Atlantic Equity Center.

Larry P. v. Wilson Riles, 495 F. Supp 926 (1979).

Lawler, J. M. (1978). *IQ, heritability, and racism.* New York: International Publishers.

Lazar, I., & Darlington, R. (1978). *Summary: Lasting effects after pre-school.* Ithaca, NY: Cornell University Press.

Levin, H. M., & Schutze, H. (Eds.). (1983). *Financing recurrent education: Strategies for improving employment, job opportunities and productivity.* Beverly Hills, CA: Sage Publications.

Lezotte, L. W., & Bancroft, B. A. (1985, Summer). School improvement based on effective schools research: A promising approach for economically disadvantaged and minority students. *Journal of Negro Education, 54*(3), 301–312.

Little, R. (1968, October). Basic education and youth socialization in the armed forces. *American Journal of Orthopsychiatry, 38*(5), 869–876.

Losen, E., Orfield, G., & Daniel, J. (2002). *Racial inequity in special education.* Cambridge, MA: Harvard Education Press.

Lynn, R., & Vanhanen, T. (2002). *IQ and the wealth of nations.* Westport, CT: Praeger.

Marks, W. (1981). *Strategies for educational change: Recognizing the gifts and talents of all children.* New York: McMillan Publishing Co.

Martin, R. (1980). *Teaching through encouragement: Techniques to help students learn.* Englewood Cliffs, NJ: Prentice Hall.

Mauer, M. (1990). *Young Black men and the criminal justice system: A growing national problem.* Washington, DC: The Sentencing Project.

Mauer, R. (1992). *Caught in the middle: A leadership guide for partnership in the workplace.* New York: Productivity Press.

McClelland, D. (1990). Sources of an achievement. In D. McClelland & R. Steele (Eds.), *Human motivation.* Morristown, NJ: General Learning Press.

Mendler, A. (1992). *What do I do when? . . . How to achieve discipline with dignity in the classroom.* Bloomington, IN: Solution Tree (formerly National Educational Service).

Mercer, J., & Lewis, J. (1979). *System of Multicultural Pluralistic Assessment (SOMPA): Technical manual.* San Antonio, TX: Psychological Corporation.

Merging for their minds. (1999, November 3). *USA Today.*

Mitchell, W., & Conn, C. P. (1985). *The power of positive students: The program that is producing dramatic changes in the effectiveness of our schools.* New York: William Morrow.

Morgan, H. (1980). How schools fail Black children. *Social Policy 10*(4), 49–54.

Murnane, R. (1975). *Empirical analysis of the relations between school resources and the cognitive development of Black inner city children in a large urban school system (New Haven, CT).* Referenced in the National Institute of Education's Final Report on Schooling of Young Children: Cognitive and Affective Outcomes, 1975.

References

Murray, H. B., Herling, B. B., & Staebler, B. K. (1973). The effects of locus of control and pattern of performance on teacher evaluation of a student. *Psychology in the Schools, 10,* 345–50.

National Center for Education Statistics. (1997). *National study on parent involvement.* Washington, DC: U.S. Department of Education.

National Center for Education Statistics. (2001). *Common core of data (CCD): Local education agency universal dropout and completion data file for school year 2000–01.* Washington, DC: U.S. Government Printing Office.

National Commission on Teaching and America's Future. (1996). *What matters most: Teaching for America's future.* New York: Author.

National Committee for Citizens in Education. (1975). *Public testimony on public schools.* Berkeley, CA: McCutchcan.

National Education Association. (2003). *Recruitment and retention of minority educators.* Washington, DC: Author.

National Urban League. (1992). *State of Black America.* New York: Author.

National Urban League. (2000). *State of Black America.* New York: Author.

Nieto, S. (1996). *Affirming diversity: The sociopolitical context of multicultural education.* New York: Longman.

Nisbitt, U. (1990). *Mega trends.* New York: Morrow.

Nord, C. W. (1997). *Fathers' involvement in their children's schools: National household education survey.* Washington, DC: U.S. Department of Education, Office of Educational Research and Improvement, National Center for Education Statistics.

Oakes, J. (1986, September). Keeping track, part 1: The policy and practice of curriculum inequality. *Phi Delta Kappan, 68*(1), 12–17.

O'Brien, M., & Little, C. (Eds.). (1990). *Reimaging America: The arts of social change.* Philadelphia: New Society Publishers.

Olsen, G., & More, M. (1982). *Voices from the classroom.* Oakland, CA: Citizens Policy Center.

Orfield, G. (2001). *Raising standards or raising barriers: Inequalities and high stakes testing in public education.* New York: Century Foundation Press.

Orfield, G., & Gordon, N. (2001, July 19). School segregation on the rise. *Harvard University Gazette.* Available at: www.news.harvard.edu/gazette/2001/07.19/12-segregation.html (retrieved August 27, 2003).

Parker, W., & Parker, R. H. (1981). I ain't no group, I'm me. In W. Marks and R. Nystrand (Eds.), *Strategies for educational change* (pp. 49–62). London: MacMillan Press.

Pear, R. (1991, January 10). Rich got richer in the 80s; others held even. *New York Times*, p. A1.

Perez, S. (1999). *State of Hispanic America: Moving up the economic ladder: Latino workers and the nation's future prosperity.* Washington, DC: National Council of La Raza.

Perkins, U. E. (1975). *Home is a dirty street: The social oppression of Black children.* Chicago: Third World Press.

Radford-Ruether, R. (1983). *Sexism and God talk: Toward a feminist theology.* Boston: Beacon Press.

Ravitch, D. (2000). *Left back: A century of failed school reforms.* New York: Simon & Schuster.

Reeves, J. *Clear board and superintendent roles are crucial to the district.* Association of Alaskan School Boards. Available at: www.aasb.org/board_superintendent.html (retrieved August 27, 2003).

Rist, R. (1972, October). Social distance and social inequality in a ghetto kindergarten classroom. *Urban Education, 7*(3), 241–261. (ERIC Document Reproduction Service No. EJ067331).

Rist, R. (1978). *Study of how teachers treat children differently.* Referenced in the National Institute of Education's Final Report on Schooling of Young Children: Cognitive and Affective Outcomes, 1978.

Rosenthal, R., & Jacobson, L. (1968). *Pygmalion in the classroom: Teacher expectations and pupils' intellectual development.* New York: Holt, Rinehart and Winston.

Sadker, D., & Sadker, M. (1985, January). Is the O.K. Classroom O.K.? *Phi Delta Kappan, 66,* 358–361.

Sadker, M., Sadker, D., & Long, L. (1989). Gender and educational equality. In J. Banks and C. A. McGee (Eds.), *Multicultural education: Issues and perspectives.* Boston: Allyn & Bacon.

Samuels, C. A. (2000, February 7). New teachers, wise mentors: Recent graduates get help, encouragement. *The Washington Post,* B1.

Scheider, B., Shiller, K., & Coleman, J. (1988). *Public school choice? Some evidence from the National Education Longitudinal Study.* Washington, DC: NELS.

Scott, M. K. (2003). Exploring intragroup conflict constructs and behaviors of African American public school children in an inner-city conflict resolution education (CRE) program. *Conflict Resolution Quarterly, 21*(1).

Shakur, T., & Pizzaro, T. (1995). *Dear mama.* On Me against the world. Santa Monica, CA: Interscope.

References

Shonk, J. (1992). *Team-based organizations: Developing a successful team environment.* Homewood, IL: Irwin Professional.

Silberman, C. (1971). *Crisis in the classroom.* New York: Vintage Books.

Sine, T. (1991). *Wild hope.* Dallas: Word Publishing.

Sivanandan, A. (1999, February 24). *What is institutional racism?* Guardian Newspapers Limited, D1.

Smiley, T. (2002). *How to make Black America better.* New York: Anchor Books.

Smith, R. P., & Denton, J. J. (1980, Spring). The effects of dialect, ethnicity, and orientation to sociolinguistics on the perception of teaching candidates. *Educational Research Quarterly, 5,* 70–79.

Smith, W. C. (1985). *The church in the life of the Black family.* Valley Forge, PA: Judson Press.

Snyder, T. (1999). *Digest of education statistics.* Washington, DC: National Center for Education Statistics, U.S. Department of Education.

Snyderman, M., & Rothman, S. (1988). *The IQ controversy, the media and public policy.* New Brunswick, NJ: Transaction Books.

Southerland, D. (1999). *Transitioning.* Grand Rapids, MI: Zondervan Press.

Survey of America's youth shows importance of job shadowing in making realistic career choices. Available at: www.jobshadow.org (retrieved January 25, 2002)

Tatum, B. D. (1997). *Why are all the Black kids sitting together in the cafeteria?: And other conversations about race.* New York: Basic Books.

Taylor, O. (1987). *Cross-cultural communication: An essential dimension of effective education.* Washington, DC: Mid-Atlantic Equity Center.

Thernstrom, A. M., & Thernstrom, S. (2003). *No excuses: Closing the racial gap in learning.* New York: Simon & Schuster.

Tonoli, T. (2001, Summer). The Pipeline Project. *Teaching and Change, 8*(4),367–369.

Urice, J. (1989, May/June). The next century: The impact of social and economic trends on the arts in education. *Design for Arts in Education,* 37.

U.S. Census Bureau. (2000). *Statistical abstracts of the United States: 1989.* Washington, DC: U.S. Government Printing Office.

U.S. Census Bureau. (2000). *Statistical abstracts of the United States, 1999.* Washington, DC: U.S. Government Printing Office.

U.S. Department of Education. (1998). *Office of Civil Rights, elementary and secondary civil rights survey: Conditions of education.* Available at: nees.ed.gov/pubs/condition98/c9843d01.html

U.S. Department of Education. (2000). *Local education agency report: Dropout and completion data file, school year 1999–2000.* Available at: Colorado.edu/education/BUENO/crede/intro.html

U.S. Department of Education, Elementary & Secondary Education Office for Civil Rights. (1993). *Civil rights compliance reports, 1992.* Washington, DC: U.S. Government Printing Office.

U.S. Department of Justice. (2001, May). *Study of men age 20–29.* Washington, DC: U.S. Government Printing Office.

U.S. Department of Labor, Bureau of Labor Statistics. (2002). *Unemployment in the United States.* Washington, DC: U.S. Government Printing Office.

Valient, B., & Hill, C. (1992, March). *ASCD Conference Greetings.* Presented at the ASCD Annual Conference, New Orleans, LA.

Walberg, H. (1984, February). Families as partners in educational productivity. *Phi Delta Kappan, 65*(6), 405–409.

Washington, V. (1982, Winter). Racial differences in teacher perceptions of first and fourth grade pupils on selected characteristics. *The Journal of Negro Education, 51,* 60–72.

Weaver, R. (2003, December 15). *One size does not fit all.* National Education Association Radio Spot. Washington, DC.

Weinberg, G., & Catero. H. (1971). *How to read a person like a book.* New York: Hawthorn Books.

Weissman, J. (1998, Fall). A study of White, Black, and Hispanic students: Transition to a community college. *Community College Review, 26,* 19–42.

Williams, F., & Miller, L. (1972, Spring). Relations between language attitudes and teacher expectancy. *American Educational Research Journal,* 263–277.

Wittmer, J. (1992). *Valuing diversity in the schools: The counselor's role.* Washington, DC: Office of Educational Research and Improvement.

Wright, J. (2003, March 23). In the Temple: Truth vs. Tradition. Lecture series presented at the Trinity United Church of Christ, Chicago, IL.

Make the Most of Your
Professional Development Investment

Let Solution Tree (formerly National Educational Service) schedule time for you and your staff with leading practitioners in the areas of:

- **Professional Learning Communities** with Richard DuFour, Robert Eaker, Rebecca DuFour, and associates
- **Effective Schools** with associates of Larry Lezotte
- **Assessment for Learning** with Rick Stiggins and associates
- **Crisis Management and Response** with Cheri Lovre
- **Classroom Management** with Lee Canter and associates
- **Discipline With Dignity** with Richard Curwin and Allen Mendler
- **PASSport to Success** (parental involvement) with Vickie Burt
- **Peacemakers** (violence prevention) with Jeremy Shapiro

Additional presentations are available in the following areas:

- At-Risk Youth Issues
- Bullying Prevention/Teasing and Harassment
- Team Building and Collaborative Teams
- Data Collection and Analysis
- Embracing Diversity
- Literacy Development
- Motivating Techniques for Staff and Students

Solution Tree

304 West Kirkwood Avenue
Bloomington, IN 47404
(812) 336-7700
(800) 733-6786 (toll free)
FAX (812) 336-7790

NEED MORE COPIES OR ADDITIONAL RESOURCES ON THIS TOPIC?

Need more copies of this book? Want your own copy? Need additional resources on this topic? If so, you can order additional materials by using this form or by calling us toll free at (800) 733-6786 or (812) 336-7700. Or you can order by FAX at (812) 336-7790 or visit our website at www.solution-tree.com.

Title	Price*	Qty	Total
From Rage to Hope, Second Edition	$ 23.95		
Achievement for African-American Students	21.95		
A MentorActive Approach to Reclaiming Youth At Risk (audiocassettes)	139.00		
Building Classroom Communities	9.95		
Building Cultural Bridges (leader's guide and student workbook)	149.00		
Reclaiming Youth At Risk	23.95		
Reclaiming Our Prodigal Sons and Daughters	18.95		
Respecting Diversity in the Classroom (video and facilitator's guide)	195.00		
Whatever It Takes	24.95		
	SUBTOTAL		
	SHIPPING		
Continental U.S.: Please add 6% of order total. Outside continental U.S.: Please add 8% of order total.			
	HANDLING		
Continental U.S.: Please add $4. Outside continental U.S.: Please add $6.			
	TOTAL (U.S. funds)		

*Price subject to change without notice.

❑ Check enclosed   ❑ Purchase order enclosed
❑ Money order   ❑ VISA, MasterCard, Discover, or American Express (circle one)

Credit Card No._____ Exp. Date_____
Cardholder Signature _____

SHIP TO:

First Name_____ Last Name_____
Position _____
Institution Name_____
Address_____
City_____ State_____ ZIP _____
Phone_____ FAX_____
Email _____

304 West Kirkwood Avenue
Bloomington, IN 47404
(812) 336-7700 • (800) 733-6786 (toll free)
FAX (812) 336-7790
email: order@solution-tree.com
www.solution-tree.com